Feng Shui Your Life!

Alice Inoue

Copyright © 2010 Alice Inoue
All Rights Reserved

ISBN 1439276889
ISBN-13 9781439276884

DEDICATION

To the mentors in my life who have inspired me

SPECIAL ACKNOWLEDGMENT

Alan—I credit you fully for pointing me towards feng shui as a career and for supporting me through all my learning years into the present. I would not be where I am if it wasn't for you. You truly bring inspiration into my life every day, and for this I am thankful.

ACKNOWLEDGMENTS

Sarah Aschenbach—I will never do a book without you! Your editing brings out the best in what I write. Every reader benefits from your incredible talent and the magical way you shape my words. Thank you, Sarah!

Gay Dochin—Thank you for being such a big part of this book, from helping me create the cover design and diagrams to preparing the final manuscript. Your talents as my designer and webmaster are invaluable! I am so appreciative of your friendship and your presence in my life.

Arna Johnson and Geralyn Camarillo (aka "Sophia" and "Shimmie")—Your beautiful Uluart images have graced my life and my website for so many years and now I thank you for the honor of having Uluart on the cover of my book! I appreciate your friendship, your love and all that we share. May ululart.com continue to be an incredible success blessing the lives and homes of many!

SPECIAL THANKS

Judy Segawa, Marie-Jose Noyle, Kelly Sugano, Erin Ushijima—My talented team members. Thank you from the bottom of my heart for always being there to help me move through each day! I love the special bond I share with each of you.

Clients, Friends, and Family—You have enriched my life in so many ways. Thank you for your presence in my life.

A NOTE TO THE READER

Molly Malone is a fictitious character and is not in any way, shape, or form based on any person, past or present. I created her persona specifically for the purpose of this book. In addition, the names of the people mentioned as examples have been changed or omitted for reasons of confidentiality. In some instances, different situational scenarios were created to further protect their identities. Any details or circumstantial similarity to you or someone you know is purely coincidental. In all cases, however, the examples faithfully reflect the core concepts that I want to convey.

TABLE OF CONTENTS

Preface	i
Introduction	iii
Meet Someone Special: Molly Malone	vi
How to Use This Book	xi
Chapter One: Your External Environment	1
Understanding Outer Feng Shui	
Chapter Two: Your Internal Environment	9
Understanding Inner Feng Shui	
Chapter Three: Lifework	19
It's All About You	
Chapter Four: Alice's Feng Shui Basic Rule #1	45
Minimize Clutter	
Chapter Five: Alice's Feng Shui Basic Rule #2	61
Have Things You Love Around You	
Chapter Six: Alice's Feng Shui Basic Rule #3	71
Pay Attention to the Pictures on the Wall	
Chapter Seven: The Five Elements	79
Yin-Yang and the Five Elements	
Chapter Eight: The Feng Shui Bagua	101
Defining Nine Areas of Your Life	
Family	
Wealth and Abundance	
Health	
Helpful People and Travel	
Children and Creativity	
Knowledge	
Reputation	
Career	
Marriage and Partnership	

Chapter Nine: Feng Shui Hot Topics   **135**
    Frequently Asked Questions

Chapter Ten: Empower Yourself   **155**
    The Journey of Your Life

Molly Today...   **160**

Appendix: **163**
    Recommended Feng Shui Books,
    Websites, Schools, Practitioners

About the Author   **165**

PREFACE

As a feng shui practitioner, I have seen firsthand the positive effects that feng shui can have on one's life when it is applied to the environment. When used with intention in our homes and businesses, feng shui has the potential to lead us towards manifestation on many levels of our lives. Not long after I started my business of feng shui consulting, however, I found that sometimes even using feng shui does not change a person's life circumstances in the desired way.

Because of this, the concept of "inner feng shui" took form quite early in my career as I recognized that applying feng shui to the environment is not enough to cure everything we are dissatisfied with. I saw that we have to take responsibility for what we have created and make different choices in order to see a lasting change. How to go about doing this in the most efficient and effective way, then, became my point of focus.

Over the years, I have taken part in an uncountable number of self-improvement courses, motivational sessions, self-help seminars, personal development workshops, life empowerment classes, and spiritual sessions in search of a method, a technique, or a way to help myself "align" what was going on within me to obtain what I desired to manifest in my life—and to help others do that, too.

It wasn't until I was introduced to the work of Dr. John Demartini that I found what I was looking for (*www.drdemartini.com*). Through his life's work as a researcher, scientist, philosopher, teacher, and writer, he has studied human potential and developed proven methods to equilibrate, or balance, the mind in order to break through to new levels. After taking two of his intensive courses and finding great value in his teachings, I attended his yearly class titled "Master Planning for Life," where we asked ourselves over two thousand questions. The answers I found gave incredible clarity and purpose to my life.

As a result of that class, I saw that self-questioning is the way to get the answers we need to make choices that enable us to move forward in the most authentic way. Couple that with using feng shui in your environment for external support and reinforcement, and you have the best possible combination of methods for creating immediate and lasting change, because you are focusing on both the "outer" and the "inner" — two parts of a whole.

Chapter Three contains questions for you to ask yourself and was inspired by Dr. Demartini's class. The questions and concepts presented in regards to purpose, values, uniqueness, and inspiration that form the basis for Chapter Three is extremely valuable to address. Although some questions are not unique within themselves, asking them in succession and recording the answers for later contemplation will bring forth an immensely powerful awareness.

Although I coined the term "inner feng shui," by which I mean the process of aligning body, mind, heart, and spirit, the word *Lifework* was introduced to me by my friend and chiropractor, Dr. Chad Sato. I use it in place of the term *homework*. *Lifework* sounds so much more inspirational than the image of drudgery brought up by the word *homework*.

My wish for you is that you spend as much time on your inner feng shui as you do on your outer feng shui and see the importance of both. I have found that combining the two is truly the way to "feng shui your life" and create the life that you are here to live.

INTRODUCTION

Due to the nature of my work, I see a lot of different people from all walks of life. As well as clients, this includes friends, vendors, neighbors, and new people I have the opportunity to meet throughout the course of a day. If they happen to ask me what is keeping me busy, I usually mention that I am in the midst of writing a book, because when I am in writing mode, it consumes so much of my time and energy that it's all I can think or talk about.

In the course of conversation, they invariably ask me what I am writing about. When I tell them my topic is "how to feng shui your life," immediately almost everyone exclaims some variation of, "Oh, my goodness, that is exactly what I need!" or "That's just what my husband/friend/boss needs!" We all have a good chuckle, and even if the words are said in jest, at some level there is a part in all of us that desires a life that is "better" in some way than what it is.

These days, practically everyone knows that feng shui has something to do with shifting your environment in order to create balance, harmony, and flow in your life. I rarely run across anyone who hasn't heard of it. People who are open to trying something different in their lives are drawn to it because they hope that shifting things around in their environment will make positive shifts in their lives.

As a feng shui practitioner, consultant, and teacher of this amazing philosophy, I have seen firsthand how a more balanced environment can impact its inhabitants in a tangible way—everything from improved finances and an increase in business clients to new love relationships and better health. What drew me to feng shui was the possibility that I could help to positively affect someone's life experience by realigning the unseen energetic vibrations of the environment in which that person lived.

Over the course of consulting for clients and following up on the results, however, I have noticed that the environment can change someone's life circumstances only up to a given point. After that, it is up to the person to take the next level of responsibility in creating the changes they desire.

Whenever I am asked, "Can feng shui help influence positively what's going on in my life?" my answer is a wholehearted yes. However, I discourage those who seem to be holding on to a fantasy that feng shui will magically "cure" their hardships— because they will be disappointed.

In feng shui, there is a maxim: "as within, so without." When I go to a home or business, I can immediately see how the people living or working there are energetically experiencing the environment and in what area they are likely having challenges. To a trained practitioner, the expression of an environment can be easily read, because the symbolism of what is going on within a home mirrors what is going on in the occupants' lives.

Using feng shui to make changes to an environment can help to create supportive energy that will aid in balancing the perceived challenges and bringing more ease and flow to a person's life. However, there is a limit to what feng shui can do. The occupants must be willing to participate further by making necessary changes within themselves in order for true change to occur.

As an example, a woman I'll call Jennie asked me to work with her to create a more peaceful home environment. At the consultation, I found out that a "peaceful home environment" really meant that she wanted to reduce her husband's yelling and temper tantrums. After she made some balancing feng shui changes to her home, she noticed that he seemed somewhat "calmer," but he was still yelling—just not as often.

She called to ask me what "advanced" feng shui advice I could give her to minimize his yelling. My answer was that she should encourage him to seek therapy. I explained to her that the environment could not do all the work for him; for change to happen, he had to want to change. Likewise, I advised her that it was also important for her to focus on herself and her own choices: what was she willing to put up with?

What I want to emphasize is that you can feng shui your environment and it will definitely create a better source of visual and energetic support, but it will *not* change your life. To change your life, you will have to make different choices. You can use your environment to help you get started, but

Introduction

when it comes down to it, you are the only one who can alter the reality of your life.

To help you with this, each chapter includes Lifework that addresses the balance and alignment of your body, mind, heart, and spirit—or what I call your "inner feng shui." Asking yourself specific questions and becoming aware of how you are aligned within is a vital component to understanding how to live a life filled with heartfelt dreams, desires, hopes, and visions.

Our challenges sometimes feel like random happenings outside ourselves, things that are caused by the people or circumstances in our lives. While it is natural to blame these outside situations for the physical, emotional, or mental chaos we experience, in reality it is our own lack of clarity that causes us to perceive our lives as we do and make them what they are.

If you don't take the time to empower yourself by defining what it is you want in your life, the Universe helps you along by bringing situations that challenge you to awaken to a new path or perspective.

We all have challenges. That is how we grow and evolve as human beings. However, it is so much easier to face challenges when you are on a path you choose to be on instead of one you are living by default. The more uninspired you are, the more disempowered you are, and the more challenges you perceive you have. This is because you have moved away from living your life according to the authentic "you." Your "inner feng shui" is out of alignment with your true self.

I hope you will use this book as a guide and devote countless hours to creating a supportive environment for yourself using "outer feng shui" while you are discovering who you are using "inner feng shui." Put your heart and soul into finding all aspects of who you are. Look without, look within, and make conscious changes: this is what it means to "feng shui your life."

When you are true to who you are, you operate from your heart. When you step forth from your heart, the Universe moves heaven and earth in order to create opportunities to help you fulfill your purpose and your destiny. When you have a clear vision, your inspired actions will produce amazing results.

Feng Shui Your Life is an entry point to the pathways you will take to your desired destinations as you journey through life. There is nothing better than getting inspired about yourself and creating an environment that supports you in making the changes you want. Get ready for a journey of commitment to *you*, and let's "feng shui your life" together!

As we begin, you are about to meet someone: Molly Malone, a woman who decided to step on the path of empowerment and make changes in her life in order to master her own destiny. We will follow her journey throughout the book and see how she uses the information presented here to create a life that is more authentic to who she is.

Meet Someone Special: Molly Malone

Molly Malone is a woman I created who appears throughout this book. Her thoughts, emotions, and actions are based on a collection of my most typical client stories. I created her as a way to express a broad spectrum of information more congruently, yet still offer real-life client experiences as examples you can benefit from.

Throughout this book, you will follow Molly's journey as she learns about feng shui. You'll get to know Molly as a person—her background and the bigger picture of her life—and see how she applies outer feng shui to her environment and inner feng shui to her life. You will be able to see through her eyes how she uses feng shui concepts, one by one, to empower herself on all levels—from the physical to the spiritual and everything in between. This, I believe, will give you a fuller idea of what it means to feng shui your own life.

I hope that Molly's presence brings a special energy into your experience of this book. Although she is a fictitious character, she may at times seem like a real person. That is because she is literally different aspects of real people combined into one. Maybe you will see bits and pieces of yourself in Molly and will be able to relate to her thoughts, her feelings, and her life challenges. I know I certainly did.

Introduction

Molly's life

Molly is a lovely brunette woman in her mid-forties who was ready to give up hope that her life could ever be different or that she could ever be happy. She has a stable yet hectic job in copier sales for a large company. Her husband, Mackie, works for an engineering firm, and they own a nice home in a convenient area of town. As we begin her story, she feels stressed out, overworked, challenged, overwhelmed, frustrated, and short-tempered at times. "But who isn't, these days?" she tells herself.

Although Molly has always given her time and energy to help others and is kept very busy with her life, she is constantly aware of an empty feeling deep down inside that never goes away. She can't put her finger on the exact reason she feels this way, yet in the rare moments when she is honest with herself, she admits that she is unhappy and that her life is not inspiring to her. She feels that she is on a never-ending treadmill and has lost control.

Unhappy with Her Life

Whenever Molly starts thinking too much about her life, she worries about getting older, about her job and her future, about wasting her life, and about many other things, and then she gets depressed. This is not the life she wanted to live. Years ago, she frequently talked to her husband about how she was feeling. Finally, he had enough and said to her, "Molly, you should be grateful for what you have. There are others who have lost their jobs and their homes and are out on the street. Consider yourself lucky and focus on what you *do* have in your life. You should go talk to a professional; maybe there's something wrong with you."

That was exactly it. Something was wrong with her and she didn't know what it was. At the time, she figured that her husband was probably right—she needed to talk to a professional and get a new perspective, so she made an appointment to see a Dr. Steven Stussey, based on a glowing recommendation from a co-worker.

Molly Seeks Help

Molly was surprised to discover that Dr. Stussey was a psychiatrist (not a psychologist as she had assumed), but he seemed like a nice man and he immediately settled her mind by telling her that her feelings were normal.

He prescribed something he said would help her to manage the undesirable emotions and the mental stress she was experiencing. She was hesitant at first, but he made it sound so normal. Besides, he said the medication would help her not feel so overwhelmed by life, so she decided to give it a try.

It was true: taking the medication helped her cope with her life much better and disengage from her emotions more easily, and as a result, she felt happier and more balanced.

A Surprise Occurrence

That is, she felt better until someone stole her purse from the front seat of her car when she was filling up her gas tank. After she had dealt with the immediate concerns, she realized with a start that the bottle of pills was in her purse. "Oh, well," she thought, "when I get to the office I'll just call for another prescription."

She discovered that Dr. Stussey was out of town for three weeks, and after calling the referring doctor's office, she found that the doctor could not refill the medication without meeting with her first. Although there was a two-week waiting period, Molly made the appointment, figuring she would be all right. After all, it was "only" two weeks.

Well, it was worse than she could ever have imagined. Everything in her life that was irritating, frustrating, frightening, or stressful was gradually magnified. Her impatience, fluctuating moods, and unhappiness came back with a vengeance. She suddenly realized that nothing had changed. The medication was only masking what was really going on inside. She didn't want to be on medication for the rest of her life, but she didn't know what else to do.

Sharing with Her Best Friend

Over a Lemon Drop martini on a Friday night with her best friend, Julie Jacobs, what was supposed to be a fun night to "get away from it all" turned out to be a night filled with emotions. Molly couldn't help herself: she started crying. "Oh, Julie, I don't know what to do. There are things I used to want in my life, but I just don't know how to get them. I don't even know who I am anymore. I feel like I have lost myself. I'm a total mess. I hate my life."

Introduction

Julie hadn't realized that Molly had gotten to this point, but as Molly was talking, she got an idea. She saw that Molly definitely needed to redirect her focus, so she asked, "Have you ever heard of feng shui?" Molly had, but she didn't know much about it. Julie explained that, from what she knew, it was about the environment and the energy that you create there in order to make things flow better. Julie said she knew it had helped her cousin and her co-worker, and she suggested Molly look into it.

At that point, Molly was open to trying anything. What did she have to lose? It would be nice to have something different to focus on for a change. Something about the idea felt "right," and it was as if a ray of light broke through her inner clouds.

A Trip to the Bookstore

First thing the next morning, Molly went to the bookstore. She saw it as a "sign" that she was on the right track when she walked in and saw they were featuring a book called *Feng Shui Your Life*, by Alice Inoue. Without even browsing through the other books, she knew it was exactly the book she wanted to buy.

The timing couldn't have been more perfect. Mackie was out of town on a business trip, and she had the weekend to herself for the first time in a long time. The Universe was on her side. She couldn't wait to get into feng shui—maybe there was hope for her, after all.

Settling in at Home

When Molly got home, she took off her make-up, put on her "home clothes," unplugged the phone, and made a cup of her favorite tea. She opened the book and began reading…

"Are you ready to tap into your environment as a source of support to help you get clarity and to assist you in manifesting what you desire in your life? Do you want to be more in control of your life and how you create it? If so, feng shui may be able to help you! It is a simple tool that can be used in more than one way to help you tune you into your environment, as well as your life. If you are ready to take responsibility in an all new way and forge a new path for yourself based on positive change, read on."

Feng Shui Your Life!

    Molly couldn't help but feel this book was written especially for her. Her interest was definitely peaked and she began to feel a glimmer of hope for the first time in a long time. She took a sip of tea and couldn't wait to start. And the book actually had instructions! She enthusiastically turned the page.

How to Use This Book

This is a unique book that requires using all four levels of your being—body, mind, heart, and spirit—if you want to get the most out of it. More than a workbook, it is a "life book" that offers not only feng shui tools that you can implement in your environment to support favorable changes, but also guidance into a deeper level so that you can create lasting change and fulfillment. The questions and exercises throughout the book lead you towards deep introspection and, as a result, you will connect to your heart and your being in an all-new way. Getting clear on who you are is the first step to empowerment.

If you make a full commitment to experience this book at all levels, you will gain immense clarity about who you are, what you want, and how to create the life you want to live. Your courage will be born from inspiration, and you will live your life with a whole new awareness.

Step One

Before you begin, obtain a pen and a blank notebook, and keep them with this book.

Step Two

Start reading. You may want to just read through the book in a leisurely manner, first. Starting at Chapter Four (Alice's Feng Shui Basic Rule #1), you may want to make notes in your notebook as you go along about the things in your environment that you want to change, move, or remove. There is great value in making even a few simple adjustments to your environment according to the feng shui information in this book. You will feel a noticeable difference when you do.

By writing down things that you want to do to your space, you will save yourself from having to remember what to do after you close the book. Your notes will become a reference and an instant to-do list when you are ready to take action. Just jot down the feng shui ideas and concepts that resonate with you as you visualize the changes to specific areas of your home or office, and then do them when you feel inspired to do so.

When you get to the Lifework portions that address your inner feng shui, read through them with an open heart. Ponder the exercises and questions to gently begin the process of getting to know yourself again. See how Molly has answered some of the questions and reflect on the topics to prepare for when you decide to work on them in more depth.

After you have read through the book once and created your to-do list of the changes that you would like to make to your outer environment, you are ready for Step Three. You do not have to complete the physical changes in your environment before you go on. Just keep the notebook with your notes as a guide for when you are ready to actively work on your home.

Step Three

This is where the magic truly happens. By focusing on the Lifework portions of the book, you will be embarking on a journey into the center of your heart, remembering things about yourself that you have forgotten, being truthful with yourself, writing down visions grounded in reality about what you would like your life to be, and creating strategies to move you to an empowered place where you will be able to make it all happen.

Preparation for doing the Lifework

Schedule a few hours of "me" time in a comfortable place without phone, television, or people distractions. All you need is this book and a clean notebook and a pen, or even better, a laptop computer. Make yourself a cup of your favorite beverage.

Center yourself

Before you begin, get comfortable, close your eyes, and take a deep breath. Take a few moments to express appreciation for all that you have in your life, acknowledging that every single thing in your life (even the perceived challenges you are facing) is serving a purpose. Though you may not see the reasons at this time, open your heart and trust that, at some point, you will understand.

Commit to finding the true desires of your heart. Be open to new revelations. Let yourself know that you are ready to take your life to a new level, find a new purpose, and step into conscious awareness of your choices for how you live your life.

Step Four

Open the book and go directly to Chapter Three, where the first Lifework exercises appear. Open your notebook or computer, start with the first exercise, and follow the instructions.

I encourage you to use a computer because it will give you the ability to revise, save, and store your valuable answers. If you are using a notebook because it's more convenient for you or that is your preference, that's fine, too. The main thing is that you record your answers, as they will be the keys to unlocking your life's dreams.

A four-body experience

You will be using your physical body to write and your mental body (mind) to think, contemplate, and strategize. These are the two bodies we are most accustomed to and most comfortable working with. As you answer the questions, however, you will also engage your emotional body (heart) and your spiritual body (spirit) in order to receive authentic information from your inner being, or the "real you." This will assist you in finding your own unique way.

Your vision

Let this book be a guide that helps you create a vision for your life that leads to a future that most inspires you. All major areas of life are covered in this book. The most important thing to remember is that the results you see in your life will be exactly proportionate to your level of responsibility and commitment to the process.

You are the only one who will be with you for the rest of your life, so time spent with yourself in effective questioning and self-awakening directly results in an expansion of your life. Let your answers guide you as you begin to create your future anew.

Important Note

When answering the questions, spontaneously write your answers and pay close attention to how you feel as you are writing. Doing so will develop a new skill—listening to yourself.

There is no "right" or "wrong" when it comes to answering the questions. The most important thing is that you find your own creativity and your own answers. You cannot have a wrong answer if you are answering from your heart and answering in truth. When you feel uncomfortable and want to stop, push yourself to overcome the resistance and stick with it. It will be well worth it.

As you answer some of the questions and make the corresponding changes to your environment, you may notice new emotions rising up within you when you see how the choices you previously have made (or not made) have taken you away from who you are and what you want. See the benefit of this awareness; it indicates an awakening to your being and new possibilities for your life.

Do not dismiss the importance of taking the time to write down your answers. Only in this way can what is intangible in your mind, heart, and spirit become a tangible reality.

No one can live your life for you. Accept responsibility for getting what you want out of your life. Go beyond your preexisting paradigms, which have been interfering with your discovering things about yourself and your environment. Open your heart and your mind to new possibilities so that you can reap the rewards of freedom that empowerment can bring.

Chapter One
Your External Environment

Understanding Outer Feng Shui

Who doesn't want to have an inspiring life that flows with peace, harmony, love, and balance? No one that I know of wakes up in the morning and says, "Good morning, Universe! Give me challenges, arguments, a bad attitude, conflict, turmoil, and chaos!" We at least hope that we will be able to get through the day without having to encounter any of these undesirable elements.

In our hearts, I am sure we all want to experience success, new opportunities, abundance, love, and happiness so that we can feel inspired by our lives. We want fulfillment, but sometimes it seems that no matter how hard we try, the abundance we desire, the happiness we crave, the relationship we seek, or the life we dream of does not manifest. When contemplating what to do, some will look towards feng shui as a way to improve their personal world.

What is Feng Shui?

Literally translated from its Chinese characters, feng shui means *wind* and *water*. The Chinese noted that wind and water are vital elements of nature. They observed that when winds were gentle and water flowed there was a harmonious balance of energy, and that when these elements were out of balance, tornados, hurricanes, floods, and tidal waves brought forth chaos.

Derived from this concept of balance, feng shui is simply a nature-based body of knowledge that can be used to create an environment that is harmonious and peaceful rather than one that is chaotic and draining. Feng shui is a life-enhancing tool that can be used to "manage" the expression of energies in an environment in order to create a foundation from which one can more easily bring forth positive change.

Feng shui incorporates movement, color, elements, and balance into its wisdom and encompasses all forms of energy and life experience. These include, but are not limited to, art, science, philosophy, environmental psychology, ecology, interior design, ergonomics, architecture, ancient wisdom, and spirituality.

The origin of feng shui

We originally learned about this body of knowledge called feng shui from the Chinese, who used it and evolved it over thousands of years. It is part of their culture and is presented as a discipline of great wisdom. Because of this, feng shui is commonly thought of as Chinese, however it is much more universal and global than you may realize. The practice of creating balanced environments and positioning oneself powerfully in the environment has existed in many cultures throughout history.

Prior to coming to China, this path of knowledge came from Tibet by way of India, where it is still practiced today as Vastu Shastra. Even earlier, it was—and still is—practiced in Africa, where it is called Dogoto, which is literally translated as *healing without medicine*.

In looking to the Western world during this same time, we can see principles of space alignment in structures such as the Vatican in Rome and the Parthenon in Greece. Other cultures, as well, such as the Navajo Indians and the Mayans, understood the importance of properly positioning the self in the environment and living within balanced spaces.

Why some consider feng shui to be confusing

I've heard that many people who had enough interest to go out and purchase books on feng shui have become confused about how to properly arrange the environment. That's because one book tells you to face the north, another says you must use your birthday to calculate your favorable direction, and yet another encourages you to face the door and disregard direction. Whew! All these contradictions usually cause most people to give up on ever figuring out how to apply feng shui properly.

There are many different schools of feng shui, and that is what has caused the confusion. Since each school has its own way of approaching the environment, if you happened to read one book from each school, you would have had a hard time making sense of anything. So, here's a brief recap of the various schools of feng shui to help you understand its progression into what it is today.

The Schools of Feng Shui

In China, feng shui originally was used to select energetically auspicious positions for grave plots on the theory that happy ancestors were more likely to create favorable fortunes for their descendants.

From there, it has undergone several evolutions over the past few thousand years, and even today it continues to evolve. Modern technology, such as cell phones, microwave ovens, and other advanced electronic equipment that didn't exist in the days of feng shui in China, must now be taken into consideration, as these devices all emit harmful, unseen energies that become a part of the environment.

Landform school

From the positioning of grave plots was born the Landform school in Northern China, where the best home placement was determined by the safest place for protection against a harsh climate.

Compass school

The Landform school led to the development of the Compass school, where a compass was used to determine the best direction. The Compass school is considered the "traditional" school of feng shui, and the auspicious direction is based on one's birthday. One of the challenging aspects I find about this school is that when several people inhabit a space, someone has to decide whose favorable direction will be used. Confusing, indeed!

Black Sect school

The Black Sect school teaches the most recent evolution of feng shui and was brought to the United States in the 1980s by a man named Professor Thomas Lin Yun, also known as Grandmaster Lin Yun. It is also known as BTB Feng Shui (Black Sect Tantric Buddhism) and is considered the most spiritual approach for balancing the energies of an environment.

The approach offered by the Black Sect (which has nothing to do with anything black or dark) was given its name when the original mystical teachings split into five lineages. The Black Sect was simply the sect that held knowledge pertaining to the physical environment. Other colors represented other sects that held wisdom on things such as health and healing or the teachings of the great philosophers.

This school's original teachings are the foundation from which I learned, yet I continue to evolve my own knowledge, theories, and application of feng shui as I understand more about energy and the times we live in. You will see more about this evolution throughout the book as I take the principles of feng shui that we apply to the environment and apply them to the body, mind, heart, and spirit.

How Does Feng Shui Work?

One of the most frequently asked questions I encounter is, "How does feng shui work?" I usually answer this question by using the analogy of a television screen and a remote control. In the same way a remote control emits an invisible signal that causes the screen to change, so also do the things in our environment emit invisible signals that we interact with and react to. If we receive "positive" signals from the environment, we have an easier time getting inspired to take action in "positive" ways to manifest that which we desire in life.

Each thing exists in relationship to each other thing, and although the furnishings and structure in a room may appear to be solid, they give off "vibrations" that can not only be measured scientifically, but also can be sensed on a subtle level by the people in the room.

In addition, the colors, elements, shapes, pictures, and items—even dust—give off their own vibrations that add to the energetic mix. This vibratory mix can't be seen but can most definitely be felt. I call it the "unheard song" in an environment. This is why you might notice that some environments "feel" better than others, in the same way you like some styles of music better than others.

Your body speaks the language of vibration fluently, so no matter where you are, your body is "listening" to your environment and giving you constant feedback through your feelings. So, for example, if you need to get a lot of work done, it's much more energetically supportive to do it somewhere that feels open, airy, and comfortable (a higher vibration that supports you) than in a place that is poorly lit, has musty furniture, and lots of clutter around (a lower vibration that is draining).

Your External Environment

Everyone has feng shui wisdom within

Regardless of our country, culture, creed, gender, or race, we all have unrecognized feng shui wisdom within us that we tune into when setting up a space. We naturally use thoughtful placement in regards to our living environment and furnishings, whether or not we are aware of it at the time. This is the essence of feng shui.

For example, have you ever tried to find a place for something in your house and no matter where you put it, you noticed that it wasn't quite right? Finally, you decide to move something out of the way to make room and—*voila!*—it is perfect. Now, why didn't you just leave it where you first put it? Because it didn't "feel" good! So many of the things we do, we do best when we let our feelings guide us, and our environment is no exception.

Think about how you have walked into places that just "felt right" and at other times walked into places and immediately thought "Ugh!" The energetic feedback of the environment caused these feelings. You immediately sensed the vibrations of the space, or the "feng shui," even though you didn't call it that.

If you choose to stay in an environment that doesn't "feel" good, your mind has to override the signals you receive and, although you can still function, you are not utilizing your energy optimally. This is because the energy that you would have been able to use for positive creation is being spent on "ignoring" and balancing the unsupportive environmental signals. When you change the feng shui, you are able to regain use of some of the energy that you previously lost to your environment.

Trust your own feng shui ability

Over the years of working with people on their feng shui, I have learned that we all have within us the ability to read and tune into an environment. We have just forgotten how to listen. When I make suggestions during a consultation, sometimes the client's face lights up and he or she says, "That's what I was thinking of doing!" This sense is within everyone, but it takes some time to trust it as well as to develop it and coax it out. I encourage you to constantly work on "feeling" your environment and letting it "speak" to you.

Beginning Your Feng Shui Journey

Often times, feng shui is thought of as a set of rules to follow: put a mirror here, place a fountain there, sit here, or sleep there." Instead, feng shui is a way of life in which you become aware of and learn how to tune into the energies around you. In this way, you access what you already know and use that knowledge to support yourself.

However, until that point comes, it is always helpful to have some basics as well as some rules and tips to point you in the right direction. However, once you really get into it and consciously prevent your judgmental mind from taking the lead, you will get the hang of it pretty quickly.

This book covers some of the basics of feng shui. In addition, in later chapters I will cover yin/yang theory, five elements theory, and the bagua (an energetic map of the environment): three important concepts that feng shui uses to shift the energy of an environment. These will be enough to give you a good foundation.

If you are interested in analyzing your environment and delving even deeper into feng shui, please refer to one of the books I recommend at the end of this book; these cover the entire system in a thorough and detailed way. You can also hire a professional feng shui consultant to analyze your home so that you can hone in on the things that you most need to do to make a positive energetic shift in your environment. Always remember not to get caught up in the "rules" and do what feels right for you and for your space.

Chapters Two and Three will lead you into the core of what you need to do to feng shui your life as we enter into the realm of *you* and who you are. I call it inner feng shui, and this is where the potential for the greatest awareness begins.

Chapter Four is where you will begin to find tangible guidance on how to physically shift the foundational environment in which you live or work.

Often people ask me where to place a fountain to bring in more money, whether a wind chime will bring good luck, or whether they should buy a wood or glass table for "better feng shui." Small things like this won't make much of a difference in the overall energy until you take care of the bigger things, which I cover in Chapters Four, Five, and Six.

To see the energy around you shift in a big way, start with the foundation. If you are willing to take some time and do the work, you will feel an enormous difference in the energetic atmosphere that your body and senses are exposed to in every moment.

The point of feng shui

The point of doing feng shui is to avoid financing your environment with your own precious energy. The goal is to create an environment that supports you rather than drains you. When you become aware of what is not supporting you, you enter into a conscious relationship with everything around you, thereby empowering you to make different choices.

When you use what feng shui has to offer in your environment, it affects you on all levels. You will naturally feel more energetic and be more productive. By giving yourself an energetic advantage, you are able to begin operating at your optimum—at least on the physical level.

Back to Molly…how time flies when you are engaged!

Molly looked up at the clock and realized that seemingly in a blink of the eye more than an hour had passed. She took her second sip of her now cold tea while trying to process what she had read. She looked around the living room and realized that she had not given her home much thought before. This was all so new to her, but she was definitely resonating with what she had read. It was exciting to feel a new awareness of her environment and how it could assist in supporting her. Everything she had read made sense to her. She did have certain "feelings" about various places she had been, and now she couldn't wait to read and learn more.

Molly repositioned herself to get more comfortable and turned the page to begin Chapter Two. She had a strong feeling she was going to find something she needed in this next chapter, as well.

Chapter Two
Your Internal Environment

Understanding Inner Feng Shui

The feng shui in your external environment is always working in one of two ways: it is either working for you or against you. A question arises when everything is seemingly set up to work "for you" and yet you still don't see the results you are seeking. In this case, most people just assume that the feng shui is not working. I, on the other hand, tell them that the feng shui *is* working but that they may be working so hard against themselves from within that their life can't go the way they envision it, no matter how supportive the environment is.

If outer feng shui is about shifting the external environment so that the collective vibration "sings a better song," then inner feng shui is about realigning the parts that make up who you are (body, mind, heart, and spirit) so that the expression of your life can match the song of your heart.

Inner and outer feng shui are both important components in our lives. Not only do they work synergistically with each other, but they also exist as a clear reflection of one another. Your state of inner feng shui will always determine the perception of your life experience. This in turn is reflected by your outer feng shui, and vice versa.

I believe that what I call "inner feng shui" is the key and foundation to our happiness and fulfillment. The feng shui of your environment will absolutely support you in creating what you want in life. However, if you do not take the crucial step of realigning the state of your inner feng shui to be congruent with it, then no matter what you do to set up your environment, much of what you desire will remain elusive.

Feng Shui and Health

As an example, Roz Roberts, a woman in her mid-fifties, consulted with me because she had heard that feng shui could help her health. She told me she really needed my help. She had ongoing health issues, such as joint pain, acid reflux, depression, fatigue, hypertension, high blood pressure, high cholesterol, and other symptoms that stemmed from carrying quite a bit of excess weight on her body for a long time.

In our opening discussion, I could tell that she felt she had lost control of herself. This was apparent to me not just by looking at her, but also by hearing her complaints about how hard life was with all of her health issues. She was on numerous medications, and she blamed everything and everyone for her condition: from her parents and her ex-husband to her job and society. I was happy that she had called because I knew that setting up her environment would be a great first step towards a new awareness, yet I also knew that it would be far from enough to get her to the healthy state she was envisioning.

The state of Roz's home

Her environment was not particularly supportive. It contained a lot of clutter, broken items, and wall decor that was uninspiring. Her wall colors over time had taken on a sickly peachy-grey tone. In addition, she was sleeping in a disempowering position: she could not see the door from her bed, and her head was against the wall of her bathroom, which was a constant drain on her energy. We moved some furniture and took down some décor. I gave her a feng shui to-do list that she agreed to complete within a month.

In a few weeks, she called to thank me because it had been such a long time since she had felt inspired about anything. She reported that she had completed all the changes we had talked about and that she slept better, felt better, and was taking new initiative on old projects. She had more enthusiasm, energy, and zest for life, and she sounded like a different person.

I knew that the feng shui had optimized the support her environment could give her, yet I also knew that unless she made some internal shifts, it would only be a matter of time until the environment fell back into its old state again, reflecting what was going on within her. Without doing some inner work, she would little by little regress into her old, unenthusiastic patterns and wonder why the feng shui wasn't working anymore.

While I had her on the phone, I suggested that she take the time while she was feeling empowered to work with a professional so that she could use this window of opportunity to make some serious and life-changing internal shifts. I don't think she actually "heard" what I was trying to explain, but she agreed. I gave her a referral, and that was the last I heard from her.

A later glimpse of Roz

About three years later, I saw Roz from a distance. I wouldn't have noticed her except that her oversized t-shirt with bold lettering caught my eye. "Watch out! I am fresh out of antidepressants," it said, and below it was a cartoon drawing of a crazed lady. It triggered a memory of having seen that same distinctive shirt…and then I remembered! I had seen it on Roz a few years back at our consultation. I looked more closely at the woman wearing the shirt and saw it was indeed Roz, but she looked even more challenged than I remembered.

I wasn't able to make contact with her, but I knew in an instant by looking at her that she did not take herself to the next level, as I had suggested, by working on her *inner* feng shui. It confirmed for me once again that the environment can only do so much and that feng shui is not the "magic" it is sometimes purported to be.

Finding the Truth

If there is something more you desire in your life, it is likely that there is some aspect of who you are, what you want, and why you want it that you are not clear about. If your life doesn't change in the way you want it to after you have improved your outer feng shui, the next step is to explore the state of your inner feng shui and get to know what's going on inside. Otherwise, you will continue to wonder why your life is the way it is and remain in a disempowered state while waiting for an outside source to provide the "good flow" when, in truth, you are the only one who can create it. By getting to know the real you, you will be able to operate from a different base and therefore create a different life.

The Real You

So, who are you? Let's start with you as a human being. Although it may appear that you are simply a tangible physical being, you are much more than what you see, and much more than what you think and feel.

Most people generally perceive that we are all separate from one another. We are not attuned to nature and each other in the same way that animals are. By this, I mean that animals sense it when their owners are in danger or they get agitated when a tsunami or an earthquake is imminent and look to move to higher ground. We do not naturally have a built-in awareness of our oneness with the Universe unless we strive for it or unless something profound awakens us to this.

Although we may feel mostly physical in nature, actually we are spiritual beings comprised of four bodies: physical, emotional, mental, and spiritual. Each of these four bodies has a specific role and function, and they work together to create our experience and expression in life. It is important to understand these bodies so that we can better understand ourselves.

Your physical body

Your physical body is tangible and visible and serves as the vehicle by which you move through life. This is the body in which you experience your physical health; if you do not address what you have been suppressing emotionally, mentally, or spiritually, eventually it expresses itself in the body as symptoms of discomfort, sickness, or disease. What your body expresses provides a way for you to become aware of unresolved issues that you are ignoring and that are preventing you from moving to new levels.

The physical body is very important to us as human beings for one main reason: without one, there is no "you" or "me." Your spirit must have a physical body in order to experience life on earth. You experience life through your five physical senses, as well as through your other bodies.

Your emotional body

Your emotional body is associated with your right brain and is where you experience oscillating pairs of complementary emotional opposites in the form of feelings such as happy/sad, gratitude/guilt, elation/depression, infatuation/resentment, and so forth. It works in a non-logical and non-linear way and, when it is balanced (neither happy nor sad, angry nor sympathetic, elated nor depressed), it is in tune with your all-knowing spiritual body.

Your Internal Environment

Your gut instincts and intuition are experienced by the emotional body, which is always directing you towards your heart and your center. Only when your emotional body is truly centered (along with your mental body) are you able to experience moments of true grace and love.

Your mental body

Your mental body is associated with your left brain and is known as your logical mind. It is analytical, operates in linear time, and functions using memory and imagination. Any experience you have ever had is stored in the memory of your mind. When you perceive a memory to be more pleasurable than painful, or more painful than pleasurable, you label it as "good" or "bad." If you think you have done something "bad" in the past, you hold it in your mind in the form of guilt.

The mental body is not able to stay in the present moment. It constantly jumps around from past to future and often imagines a challenging future. This is what creates fear and worries that limit your possibilities for growth.

Your spiritual body

Your spiritual body, also known as your spirit, your higher self, your inner being, or your soul, is the part of you that is connected to the all-encompassing dimension of the Universe from which you came. Your spiritual body is connected to everything and everyone and knows no limits. It knows that you are here on earth to gain experiences and to grow and evolve, and it knows your purpose. Your spiritual body is directly connected to your emotional body. It is where your inspiration, purpose, intuition, knowing, innermost wishes, and desires originate.

Body, mind, heart, and spirit

I refer to these tightly interwoven yet very individual parts of us as our body, mind, heart, and spirit. When you are not in tune with or are suppressing one or more of these bodies, you operate in an out-of-balance way. This shows up in your life as chaos, frustrations, difficulties, and often an underlying sense of feeling unhappy, which is the Universe's way of letting you know that one or more of your bodies is out of balance.

When you are on the path of self-discovery and working on your inner feng shui, you are literally heading back along the pathway to the level of consciousness from which you came before you appeared as a physical human being. By consciously working towards becoming more balanced in your total being, you will be able to more easily embrace challenges and understand your best options.

It's important to keep reminding yourself that your brain and your body are not who you are; the "real you" is your spirit, which functions through the filter of who you think you are.

The Realm of Inner Feng Shui

"Who am I?" Have you ever seriously asked yourself this question and listened to the answer that comes from within? Deep within your being, you have dreams, desires, hopes, and visions, as well as a definite purpose for being here on earth. Do you ever look at your life, wonder how you got to this point, and think that somewhere along the way you must have gotten off-track? If you feel as though you are lost in some way, it is simply that you have strayed from the connection with your body, mind, heart, or spirit.

When you are out of touch with your deeper self, it is common to feel restless or dissatisfied with your life. Sometimes when your inner feng shui is misaligned, it shows up as an indefinable unhappiness in your heart, the origin of which you just can't figure out, or you may feel that life has lost its zest in some way and become humdrum.

When you are not living a life that is inspiring to your being, things feel somehow "off." This is due to a lack of balance in your body, heart, mind, or spirit.

How do we get off-center?

Most of us are raised to subordinate ourselves to a set of rules imposed on us by outside authority figures, such as parents, teachers, cultures, or the society in which we live. Because of this conditioning, we judge our feelings as "wrong" if they are contrary to what these perceived authorities stand for. These perceived authorities show up in your mind as the critical "inner voice" that speaks up against you any time you do something that you really want to do. It makes you feel guilty.

Your Internal Environment

When you suppress your individuality and subordinate yourself to perceived authorities, you are operating under a false set of rules and end up living contrary to your authentic self. We do this for the sake of fitting in, yet when we get too far off-center, we literally feel "off" and not ourselves.

Your inner voice

Do you remember times in your life when you did or said something and your parents or another "authority" asked you to stop or to keep quiet? Then, as you became older, you did it to yourself by putting an imaginary finger to your heart and saying "Shh" to your true desires.

In some area, we all have subordinated ourselves to a set of rules that we follow in regard to what is possible in life or what it means to be successful, or what it means to be a good parent, child, employee, sibling, community member, and so on. When our heart speaks up through our intuition and says something contrary to these internal rules, we tend to judge it as bad. Following the internal rules makes us think we are doing the "right thing" by keeping the peace, yet we don't realize that we are, in fact, sacrificing and betraying ourselves at our core by ignoring things that are important to our being.

When you go through life doing what you think you "should" do based on an outside set of rules, you become disempowered in those areas.

Listening to yourself

Isn't it interesting that when we befriend someone, we spend time with them and get to know their wants and needs, and yet we tend to spend less time listening to what *we* want and encouraging ourselves to follow our own dreams? Think back to a time you met someone with whom you wanted to form a lasting friendship. How did you get to know them? You spent time with them, asked them questions—and you listened! Whenever that friend reached a crossroads in life and was torn about which direction to take, how did you advise them? Most likely, you listened to what your friend wanted and encouraged her to follow her heart, even in the face of opposition.

There is nothing better in life than feeling inspired to listen to yourself. No matter where you are in your life or how you feel about it, it's never too late to start. Now is a perfect time to commit to really getting to know you. By doing so you will point yourself in the direction of letting go of any false fronts you feel you need to keep up to please others and any tendency to hang on to old habits and beliefs that keep you from living an authentic life.

Asking the right questions

The only way to find the path back to you is to ask yourself a lot of questions, listen to the answers with an open heart, and write them down. The next chapter gives you this opportunity. No one but you knows the answers to what is right for you. This is the process of inner feng shui: uncovering the ignored or repressed aspects of your authentic self in order to align the inner with the outer in a way that is unique and inspiring to you.

If the way you are currently living is not congruent with what your heart desires in every area of your life, it is not possible to feel fulfilled. You only have a given amount of time here on earth. Do you want to come to the end of it and look back on a life of unfulfilled visions, heartache, and disappointment? If not, find out who you are and what you want, and consciously find ways to incorporate these desires into your life.

Paying attention to the signals

Your spirit, via your heart, is constantly communicating to you your heartfelt dreams, hopes, and wishes. Whenever you ignore these messages, your being will attempt to get your attention by sending you a signal. The signal might come in the form of physical discomfort, emotional turmoil, or mental stress. These symptoms show up simply to remind us about what is most important, yet instead of listening, we often use medication to numb the discomfort or we create busy-ness in order to distract ourselves or we watch television as a way to tune it all out.

Continually disregarding what these important signals are attempting to convey to you is akin to hitting the snooze button on your life. As you move further away from your heart center, you engage more easily in non-heart-centered activities and get caught up with low-priority activities, obligations, guilt, and self-imposed responsibilities. Don't allow yourself to go through the motions of living a life you're discontent with. Consciously connect this feedback to the cause by not ignoring what is most important—you!

Inner Feng Shui Starting Point

If you are ready to find out who you are, then it's time for the right questions and the big awareness that comes from answering those questions. Questions are a natural part of life. From an early age, children are curious about what they see: "Why is there a moon?" "How do flowers grow?" From there, they develop awareness of their feelings, which leads to questions such as, "Why do I have to do what I don't want to do?" And from there, even more insightful questions arise, such as, "Why are you doing that if you really don't want to?"

If we had continued our questioning and directed it towards ourselves, we would have found great awareness and life guidance in the answers. Somewhere along the line, though, we stopped being curious about who we are and why we do the things we do and began to conform to the way things were set before us.

Now, however, you can choose to make your life about living the questions and discovering the answers. When you do, you are opening the door to finding the authentic you.

A Call to Happiness

Inside every human being is a call to happiness; your purpose is to answer that call. We all have an innate wisdom within our being that is always there, guiding us, yet until we can slow down and listen, this wisdom will not come to the surface of our consciousness. By asking yourself the right questions, you honor who you are. Spend this much-needed time with yourself. Ask yourself the questions in the next chapter. Your heart knows who you are and what you are here for.

Molly Sheds a Tear

Molly felt as if this book had been written for her. She related to everything that she read and realized that, somewhere along the line, she had lost touch with who she was. Her inner feng shui was way out of alignment. As she wiped her eyes and blew her nose, she knew that she needed to work on finding herself once again. She decided right then and there to get out her computer and start doing the exercises and answering the questions. She had all weekend to reconnect with herself. Maybe there was hope for her, after all.

Chapter Three
Lifework

It's All About You

Of all the chapters, I feel that this one is the most important. If you can get clear about who you are and what you really want, then you can begin to set up your life so that it serves you on every level. In order for this chapter to be effective, you will need to take a lot of time with it, put in a lot of thought, and make a commitment to yourself.

The purpose for doing the Lifework that is presented from this point forward is to help you to bring your life into a higher state of order on all levels: body, mind, heart, and spirit. We all have dreams, hopes, wishes, and goals. This information is within us, yet access to it is elusive because we get sidetracked by daily life and lose our focus on what it is we wanted in the first place.

By asking yourself the questions, doing the exercises, and writing the Lifework answers down, you will be able to more easily hold your focus than if you try to keep everything in your head. It is the most effective and efficient way to work on your inner feng shui so that the intangible in your mind can more easily become a tangible reality for you. Do not disregard the importance of writing your answers down. It will make all the difference.

These exercises and questions are about your life journey. Your life is yours to live, but only if you know who you are. It is most important to remember that no one can live your life for you, except for you. Having a clear vision inspires action, which can produce miraculous results.

If you are ready to begin this portion, please review the instructions (How to Use This Book), which you will find just before Chapter One. Get ready to change your perspective about who you are!

Who Are You?

How do you reply when someone asks who you are? Your immediate response would likely be your name and, following that, depending on the situation and context, you would likely answer along the lines of an outer manifestation.

For example, if you are coming from a spiritual perspective you might say that you are a Christian, a Muslim, a Catholic, or a Spiritualist. An answer having something to do with your education or career would likely be that you are a college graduate, a business owner, a librarian, or a CPA. If you are making reference to your family ties or your social connections, you might say that you are a mother, a wife, a Democrat, a Rotary Club member, or a Toastmaster leader. If you are answering from the perspective of your lifestyle, you might say that you are a vegetarian, a cancer victim, an athlete, a senior citizen, or an alcoholic. If you feel the need to make reference to your finances, you might say that you are a millionaire or a coupon-cutter.

Who we think we are is often associated with our roles (mother, boss, teacher, husband), our possessions (Lexus, penthouse, country club membership), and our personality traits (funny, shy, easy-going), when in fact these are just outer manifestations.

So, ask yourself, "Who am I?" Are you a spiritual being in a physical body? A human "BE-ing" or a human "DO-ing?" Are you a bit of both or none of either? Of course, you are what you can see, hear, smell, and taste, and you are your roles, your personality, and your identity, but is there something more to you? Who are you?

There is a part of you that exists outside of your physical body. Go deep within your heart and ask yourself who you are. What is your Being? What do you love to study? What do you seek to understand? What are you inspired by? What do you feel is your task in life? What is your goal in life? Do you have one? What do you excel at?

Action

Write, "Who am I?" at the top of the page and start writing from your heart. Use the questions in the above paragraph to guide you. Start your sentences with phrases like, "I am…" "I love to…" "I seek to…" "My goal is to…" "I am inspired by…" "I excel in…" "My belief is…" Do not judge what you write; just write from your heart.

Molly took a deep breath. She knew this would be a tough exercise for her because her entire focus had been on her roles as a wife, a daughter, and an employee and on all the things she had to do to accommodate others. She didn't even know who she was anymore or even what inspired her.

She stood up, walked around the room, got a drink of water, and sat back down. When her fingers touched the keyboard, however, it felt as if another part of her had taken over.

MOLLY MALONE

Who Am I?

I am a human being who loves being around anything bright: bright people, bright places, and bright situations. I love to be in the sun. I love to feel the wind on my face and feel that there is hope. I am inspired when I help others find that hope.

I seek to know more about how to live an inspired life. Figuring out new ways to do old things inspires me. I love puzzles and the feeling of putting in the final piece. I am inspired when people thank me for introducing them to another person who helps them. I love matchmaking. I excel when I am given the freedom to do whatever I want to do in order to make something work.

I love encouraging others to find their best selves. I feel fulfilled when I help to establish connections between others. I love to connect the right person to something that is right for him or her. I love connecting with others, finding out their needs, and helping them to find what they are looking for. I excel when I am organized and am able to accomplish goals I set out for myself. My belief is that I can find my own happiness and that I have the ability to do so.

And as an afterthought, she wrote…

I love waking up to the smell of coffee, and I love watching the sun set.

"Wow!" she thought after she read what she had written. No wonder she was so unhappy. Nothing she was doing in her life remotely resembled who she was and what she loved. She sighed as she realized that she couldn't remember the last time

she woke up to the smell of coffee. She made a mental note to set the coffee timer to go off before she woke up and to make sure she left the office before dark on Monday so she could watch the sun set. At least that would be a positive change.

She was ready for the next question and read on.

Personal Life Facts

You are a special person and your life, from the moment you were born to this present moment, is exceptional. In order to recognize your uniqueness, list some facts below about yourself that apply specifically to you. No one else has the exact same combination of traits, facts, and experiences that you have. This exercise is to show you that you are special and that you have extraordinary traits and facets that make up who you are. When you are finished, read them over and over. No one in the entire world can write the same things.

Action

Fill in the answers to the categories below. Add categories as you think of them and take out the ones that you do not care to include.
Name
Birth Date
Birth Time
Birth Location
Astrological Sign
Chinese Astrological Sign
Life Path Numerology Number
Current City of Residence
Age
Ethnic Background
Father Facts
Mother Facts

Family Background (List anything you like here: siblings who have passed on, where you grew up, the meaning of your family name, etc.)
Current Status
Past Interests

Current Interests
Lifestyle (E.g., exercise regularly, meditate, eat only organic, night owl, etc.)
Languages Spoken

Your Life Line

There is great significance to every change you have encountered in your life. It is important to recognize how each of these changes has served a purpose and has been instrumental in some way to get you to where you are today. Many aspects of who you are today and where you are in your life are a result of these points along the path of your life.

Action

Make a timeline of your life up to the present year. Start it off with:
Year of Birth:
City Born In:
Name of Hospital:

Then, following the format below, list any information that is significant in your life, such as "started first grade, moved to new house, got my own room, sister was born, parents were divorced, got my first job," etc. Be as broad or as detailed as you like. You may want to go through once and get the main years logged and then go back and refine it. Be sure to reflect upon how each event helped you in your growth and evolution.
Year:
Event:

Your Purpose Statement

You are here on earth for a purpose. As you begin to take the time and make the effort to consciously recognize this, you will see that you are a unique individual with a great spirit who is here to live life in your own creative way. We all have a desire to be fully who we are so that we can live the life we have come to live. However, too often, we decide that the opinions of others are more important than our own, and before we know it, we buy into a way of living that is not authentic to who we are and end up ambling along without clarity.

The road of your life

In *Alice in Wonderland*, there is a scene where the Cheshire cat says to Alice, "When you don't know where you are going, any road will do." Without a purpose and direction, you live your life by default. When you are aware of your greater purpose, you choose the road you travel and are in control of the direction you are headed.

How does purpose show up?

You may have one purpose that can be seen in all areas of your life, or you may have many different purposes that weave throughout your life. Many think that life purpose is a particular field, a title, or a selfless interest, such as working with the homeless or with underprivileged children.

It can encompass these things, yet I believe that there is a deeper layer to our purpose, which is to find out what inspires us amidst everything in our lives, and then to have the courage to live out that inspiration, even if it means going against everything we've been taught. The reason for finding your purpose is so that you can actively use your life as a vehicle in which to authentically express who you are.

What makes you show up for life?

From 0 to 10, how alive do you feel? Zero represents a zombie state and 10 represents fully living. What is your score? The more alive you feel, the more you are living your purpose. What would make you feel more alive? Can you specifically name what inspires you to show up for life each day? For example, a seven-year-old boy may feel that his purpose in life is to accumulate a certain number of points in the video game he is playing so that he can advance to level three. His purpose is all-consuming, and it's the first thing he wants to do when he gets up and the last thing he wants to do before he goes to sleep. This purpose inspires him to show up for his life until he evolves to the next level of understanding and finds a new purpose.

Writing a purpose statement

In all of us, there is an inner desire to be fully who we are so that we can live a life we are inspired to live. When we forget this and get caught up in the voices of others who have opinions on what is important, we end up ambling along the roads of life without our own defined purpose.

Writing your own purpose statement will not only help you to discover the contribution you can make to humanity in a way that is uniquely yours, but it will form the foundation for the path that you will live from this point forward.

Finding your purpose will make it possible for you to be fulfilled in the most meaningful way. Writing out your statement will give you a reference and can be posted in areas where you spend time, a reminder to yourself about why you are here on earth.

The ego and your purpose

One thing that may come up when you are contemplating your purpose is your ego. The ego is the part of us that believes we are separate from each other. It wants to have a purpose that makes you feel special, unique, and superior to everyone else. Do not confuse your purpose with your ego; in other words, do not confuse your heart with your mind.

How the ego defines your purpose

Sometimes the ego is tricky and gives us a purpose that sounds so good that we start to think of it as truth. You can know the ego is at play if you create an illusion of who you are that is incongruent with what is true for you.

As an example, Barbara, a long-time client, decided that her purpose was to be a healer. She studied various modalities of healing and became a "healer," complete with business cards, a rented healing room, and a business telephone line. She came to me because, even after putting so much time and energy into her practice, she was getting very few appointments and wanted to explore what was preventing her from doing her "life's work," as she put it.

Thinking that she had already found her purpose, I began questioning her to see if the apparent block to her path was physical, mental, emotional, or spiritual. Was it fear of success? Was it lack of a solid business and marketing plan? Was it lack of confidence?

During the questioning process, I thought to ask her why she didn't just go down to the local hospital and volunteer her services for the Healing Touch program on her off time if she felt so strongly about being a healer.

This would be an opportunity to get extra practice and at the same time feel fulfilled in her purpose.

She resisted that suggestion so strongly that it opened another line of questioning that finally led her to her ego. She wanted to be a popular, sought-after healer and be paid for her services to prove that she was "valuable." She wanted to look good to the members of her social group, who were very spiritual and into healing and healers. She thought that if she achieved success as a healer, they would treat her with more respect.

She had allowed her ego to get so wrapped up in finding a way to look good to this group of women that it created a purpose for her that she bought into even though it did not come from deep within her heart.

Reason versus purpose

Another thing to be aware of is getting caught between reason and purpose. Having a reason for what you are doing is different from having a purpose for what you are doing. I have another client, Linda, who has worked hard for a telephone company for over twenty years, and during this time, she has received many promotions and raises. She fell into the job early in her life and had never questioned why she was doing it. She had great reasons: security, good pay, and a nice working environment, and the job offered just enough challenges to keep it interesting.

Her schedule was filled, yet she felt a sense of something missing. Her reasons for being in her job were solid, but she was not feeling a purpose for her life. After doing some Lifework and spending time questioning herself, she discovered that the moments she felt most inspired were when she was helping her family, friends, staff, or co-workers transition through challenges and constructively supporting them in their goals.

She recognized that she is good at seeing characteristics and talents in others that they don't see in themselves and is able to guide them in growing their natural skills. She was the one who many came to for advice, and she felt alive when she could help others in this way.

Purpose-driven Action

Amongst all the things she was doing in her life, once she moved into her heart and recognized what inspired her, she got ideas about how to take what she loved to the next level. She began taking classes on coaching to develop her skills professionally and is planning to propose to her current company that they hire her as a department coach after she retires from her current position. As soon as she got this idea and took action, the void she felt went away.

Look at your busy-ness

Being as busy as possible is not the purpose of life. Although being busy can be a good and productive thing, when you are busy without purpose, or when you keep busy to cover a void, it prevents the voice of your heart from coming forth to help you to find and live a purposeful life.

What is your alternate title?

What is the real work that you do? If you could cross out the title on your business card and write down one purpose (of the many) in the job that you do, what would it be? For example, a make-up artist I know is a Self-Esteem Booster to many. The bank teller I see every week is a Day Brightener for everyone who sees her. My chiropractor is a Heart-Opener, Life Facilitator, and Perspective Shifter, always prompting others to open their hearts and look at their lives in a new way. Your purpose is likely entirely different from the label or title you give yourself.

Finding words for your purpose

Your purpose is not your job, your title, your responsibilities, or your goals. Your purpose is to express yourself in your own creative way. Most important, your purpose is the reason that you exist. You are the only one who knows your purpose because it comes from deep within your soul. Asking yourself what it is and listening to the form that it comes in today will bring you one step closer to knowing who you are.

The process of pulling this information from your heart when you sit down to address the question can bring forth some fear and guilt, making you feel stuck and spaced out. You may say, "I don't know." Do not let this stop you and hold you back from finding your purpose. Do not let your mind or your ego give you superficial answers. Start by telling yourself,

"I know my purpose" and keep saying this to yourself, remembering that there is no right and no wrong about it, no good and no bad.

It may take some time to coax it out of yourself, but keep at it until your heart begins to whisper its truth. When you begin to tap into your heart energy, you will feel like it is coming from a different source entirely, and you'll know you have found it when you get chicken skin, feel a lump in your throat, and tears well up in your eyes when you read it. Do not judge what you write as good or bad or wonder if it is doable; just sit with it and know that it is true.

Today is just a starting point. What you write today will be rewritten, revised, and refined hundreds of times as you go through life and discover new aspects of yourself, so just take a deep breath and write. You will know you are on the right track when you feel tremendously inspired by what you wrote. It will just "feel right."

By sitting with yourself, you unlock access to resources that were previously dormant: greater intelligence, awareness, and consciousness. There is a lot of purpose within you, but it may be buried under a lifetime of denial and misplaced focus. Be courageous and claim who you really are.

Action

Write at the top of the page "My Purpose Statement" and then the following: "I, (your name), do hereby declare that my primary purpose in life is to… and I do this by…."

Whoooosh! All the enthusiasm Molly was feeling went straight out of her after reading about purpose. She thought to herself, "This is too much," and immediately began to make excuses about why it was time to stop. She thought, "My life is fine as it is. I'll just use the feng shui tips in this book to spruce up the house — that will be enough. Making inner changes at this point will just take too much time and effort. I'm fine."

Molly got up and walked to the window as she sorted things out in her mind. While she stood there struggling with her resistance to move forward, a song playing in the distance caught her attention. As she tuned into the familiar Michael Jackson song, she caught the words he was singing: "If you want to make the world a better place, take a look at yourself and make a change…I'm starting with the man in the mirror…"

In that instant, Molly caught a glimpse of her reflection in the window, and she knew it was now or never. It was fear that was holding her back, and she knew it was time to claim who she was and take back the reins of ownership of her own life. She needed a new path. She needed to find her purpose.

She walked back and got comfortable once again, ready to open her heart to her life. She looked back over what she had written so far about herself and took a deep breath.

Like reciting a mantra, over and over she said, "I know my purpose…I know my purpose…I know my purpose…" And then she began to write.

MOLLY MALONE

My Purpose Statement

I, Molly Malone, do hereby declare that my primary purpose in life is to live consciously and courageously, to resonate with love, and to open my heart to who I am. My purpose is to awaken the sleeping Molly within so I can make a difference in my own life and in turn affect other people's lives. My purpose in life is to be a bridge for those who need to find their way to new ground. My purpose in life is to be an example for other women who have lost themselves. If they see that I can find myself, they will see that they can, too. My purpose is to take action in ways that inspire me to grow.

I live my purpose by standing up for myself and expressing my needs, so that I can be an example to others. I live my purpose by finding the joy in making life changes that empower me. I live my purpose by choosing to create my life instead of living it by default. My purpose is to live life authentically, according to who I know myself to be, and to grow and evolve in the pursuit of the search for myself.

"Wow!" thought Molly, "Where did THAT come from?" She reread her purpose statement again and again and noticed a warm feeling inside. She was inspired, and as a result, her eyes welled up with tears. Could this really be right? Could this really be her purpose? The words seemed to have a special energy just for her, and they felt right.

She could hear her thoughts of doubt and self-judgment starting to rise up, but she consciously chose not to pay any attention to them. She had heard her heart for the first time since she was a young girl, and she wanted to honor that voice, for once.

Now it's your turn. What's your purpose?

Embodying Your Purpose Statement

Why would you love to fulfill your purpose? It is worth taking the time to think about this and "feel" the inspiration that is driving it. When you read your purpose and begin to relate to it, imagine how you would feel if you were living your purpose. Just thinking about this will open you up to possibilities for how you could go about fulfilling it.

There is no limit to the ways in which you can fulfill your purpose. If you can immerse yourself in how it would feel to fulfill your purpose, your options will expand and your choices will become more numerous.

Action

Write a paragraph or two about why you would love to fulfill your purpose. How does it feel to imagine that you are living your life in accordance with your purpose? What do you currently do that helps you to fulfill your purpose? What do you currently do that takes you away from fulfilling your purpose?

What do you imagine would be some challenges you would face if you were living a life that was fulfilling your purpose? Just because you are living a life that is in line with your purpose does not mean that it will be a bed of roses, and it is important to be aware of that. You will still have ups and downs and challenges to contend with. The difference is that when you are living a life that is in line with your purpose, you will be more inspired and have more energy and vitality, and because of this you will be more willing to embrace what comes into your life than if you were not living life from your heart.

Your Values

Every person on this earth values what he or she feels is most important. When two people value the same things, they get along more easily than two people who don't. When two people have opposing values, it can cause one to judge the other as wrong, when in fact there is no "right" or "wrong" about it. It is simply a case of different perspectives.

The more we live according to what is important to another person, the more we live contrary to who we are, which virtually guarantees an uninspired life. When you live life in accordance with what you truly value, you feel inspired, disciplined, focused, and reliable. Have you ever noticed how you always have more energy to do the things you really want to do and can't wait to do them, but when you feel you "have to" do something that you don't consider important, you have to psych yourself up for it?

Things that you don't value much are the things you tend to need outside motivation to complete. Usually, you have a harder time focusing on them, take longer to do them, and go about them in a more disorganized way than you do when it comes to things that inspire you. Think about it for a moment to see if this is true for you.

Your values as related to your purpose

The concept and study of values has been thoroughly researched and explained in great detail by Dr. John Demartini in dozens of his books and seminars, which is how I learned about values.

When your goals are aligned with what you truly value, you increase the probability that you will achieve what you want. When your goals are aligned with what is not really important to you deep down (even if you "think" it is), you end up feeling confused and unsure about your life.

For example, if your goal or purpose is to raise well-rounded children, and if this also happens to be a high value for you, then you will be inspired to do everything you can to raise your children accordingly. You will feel more willingness to embrace the time, energy, and logistical challenges along this path than you would if this goal was low on your list of values.

If this goal is low on your list of values and you spend a majority of your time and energy on your children, you will feel confused and resentful and will likely question the purpose of your actions and your life. The bottom line is that it is important to align your purpose and your goals with your values, otherwise you live an uninspired life, always doing what you think you "should" do.

Changing values

Values can change depending on where you are in life and what is going on. For example, when a woman has a baby, the baby may become her highest value as opposed to before, when career advancement was her highest value. If this is the case, she will put her career on hold with no resentment and stay home with the baby. If her husband places the same value on the importance of her staying home with the baby, there will be no conflict about it.

If, however, career advancement remained her highest value and she went back to work even though her husband placed a high value on her staying home with the baby, her husband would likely judge her actions as "bad," and they would be in conflict over what is "important."

If, in this case, the woman allows her husband to impose his values on her and gives up opportunities for career advancement, she will end up resenting both her husband and the baby. Whenever we subordinate to another's values and live our life according to someone else's rules, we disempower ourselves and move away from who we are. In a situation such as this, unless both people can take the time to see how the other's values, though different from their own, can also be a benefit to them, they will continue to be in conflict.

Your values are uniquely yours and evolve over time through experiences that come along and change them. There are no right and wrong values, only those that are important to you.

True values

When you are defining where your values lie, it is important to be clear and honest with yourself. How you live your life clearly shows you where your values lie, but our words and actions are often incongruent.

How often have you heard someone say that they value one thing, such as financial freedom, and the next thing you know they say they have purchased a limited-edition item that no one else has and are in the process of declaring bankruptcy? If the person truly valued financial freedom, as she said she did, then she would value saving money and be working on a long-term savings plan. In this example, it sounds like the person actually values social status and exclusiveness over financial stability.

So, make sure you are honest about what you truly value. And remember, there is no right or wrong answer.

Action

Think about the things that you value in life. List nine of them in order of importance, with higher-value things at the top and lower-value things towards the bottom. Some examples could be (not limited to this list): taking care of family, finances, having a nice car, having a clean home, having your own space, time with friends, career advancement, social status, a specialized lifestyle, exercise and wellness, peace and quiet, networking, health, spouse and relationship, an organized home, children, creative endeavors, helping others, learning new things, travel, new technology, private time, organization, spiritual mission, mental wisdom, etc. Everyone has a hierarchy of values. What is yours?

My highest values

1.
2.
3.
4.
5.
6.
7.
8.
9.

Look over your values once again to make sure they are really what you want from deep inside your being, and not just values that others have injected into you, which are disempowering. For example, is having a clean house something you really want as your own value that inspires you, or did you list having a clean house because your mother told you that not having a clean house is a "bad" thing? What are you saying to yourself when you think about cleaning your house? Are you saying things like, "I have to clean the house. I have got to make more time to organize my house. I ought to keep the house cleaner. I am supposed to... I should..." and so forth?

Listen to what you are saying to yourself about what you "should" or "should not" be doing. Trying to live your life according to other people's values instead of your own is frustrating. You may think of yourself as "undisciplined" when you don't do the things that you have told yourself you "should" do, when in fact you are not at all undisciplined. You are just living by what you truly feel is important, and there is nothing wrong with that.

Sometimes, without being conscious of it, we try to force our values onto others and want them to do what *we* think is important, when in fact they just want to do what *they* feel is important. When you tell people what they should and shouldn't do, you are injecting them with your values. When you say things like, "You have to... You should... You need to..." etc., you are injecting others with your values. Trying to get others to live by your values can be frustrating, as well. Just as you would find it difficult and frustrating to live by someone else's set of values, they feel the same way.

When a husband is watching television (living by his own values and being inspired by television and relaxing) and a wife says, "Harry! You should be fixing the fence instead of sitting there watching television," she is injecting him with her set of values. Is it wrong for Harry to watch television? Not for him. His wife is judging his behavior based on her set of values because she places a high value on not having broken things around the house.

Molly took a deep breath and exhaled loudly. (She noticed she was doing a lot of exhaling since she started doing the Lifework.) Values were something that she had forgotten about. Actually, she never really had time to think about what she valued; she just did what needed to be done in the moment, never paying attention to whether it was something she felt inspired to do or not. "This should be fun," she thought, and began thinking and feeling things out. She started writing...

Lifework

I value

Free time with myself with no outside demands on my time so I can do whatever I desire

> *Quality time with Mackie*
> *An inspiring and independent career*
> *Exercise, health, and wellness*
> *Keeping up with my friends and social networks*
> *Creative endeavors*
> *Financial independence*
> *Learning new things and experiencing new places*
> *My Limoges ceramic box collection*

After a lot of thought and several rounds of rewriting and reorganizing her list, Molly was finally satisfied and read on...

After you have listed your values, ask yourself if you are living a life that incorporates most of your higher values. If so, then it is likely that you are inspired by your life.

If you are not incorporating most of your higher values into your life or do not feel inspired, do the exercise below.

Action

List where you are actually spending most of your time, energy, money, thought, conversation, and focus.

1.
2.
3.
4.
5.
6.
7.
8.
9.

Molly looked over her Values List and saw that, sadly, there was nothing on her list that she currently incorporated into her life. No wonder she was so unhappy! As suggested, she began to list where she was actually spending her time, energy, and focus. She composed the following list:

1. Work related issues and challenges: people at work, boss, unfair policies, lack of appreciation, frustration
2. Family obligations: taking Mom to social activities and doctor appointments, planning the family reunion, keeping up with Mom's mail and paying her bills – basically managing Mom's life
3. Taking care of the house: bills, chores, repairs, laundry, cleaning, food shopping, etc.
4. Talking on the phone every day to Emma about her problems and dealing with her negativity
5. Running errands for work, house, and Mom
6. Worrying about how I am going to get everything done that I have to and hating my life
7. Watching TV and spacing out
8. Reading romance novels and fantasizing
9. Complaining to anyone and everyone I see about how hard life is these days and how stressed I am

Molly sighed. She felt sad because there was nothing on her list that she really liked to do, except for Numbers 7 and 8, but she really only did those things to help her manage everything she hated about what was going on. She went back to reading more on values…

Changing Values

Have you ever "failed" when you set out to achieve new goals for yourself? That is because your values at the time did not support the achievement of those goals (even though superficially you thought they did). There were hidden benefits to what you were doing that you didn't realize were working against you.

Remember how I mentioned earlier that you always have the time and energy to do the things you really want to do? If there are things that you are doing that you don't want to do anymore, you have to find reasons not to do them. What is taking most of your time, energy, and money and is something that you want to change? It is imperative to compare the benefits of various activities so that you can create a new path from within.

Jim and his changing values

A great example is Jim, a fifty-year-old acquaintance who was about forty pounds overweight. His doctor constantly told him he needed to lose weight and adopt a healthier lifestyle "or else." Jim really did want to be healthier and tried numerous times to change his diet; he even joined a health club to get into the habit of exercising.

Somehow, though, he just couldn't stay motivated, and soon he would revert to his old ways. Even though he knew that healthy food and exercise were "good" for him, they did not align with his values. Deep down, he valued the taste of high-calorie foods, the freedom to eat without restriction, the social atmosphere, and the extra time for work or for relaxing in front of the television. This is why he always "failed" when he set a goal to live a healthier life. There really wasn't enough perceived benefit to keep him going, and so his willpower would naturally dwindle as his true values took over.

Well, one day, Jim had a heart attack and was rushed to the hospital. He was immediately rushed into surgery for a triple bypass heart procedure, and he almost died. In the process of recovery, he began to see his life differently. He saw the benefits of life and the benefits of health. He felt happy to be alive. He saw the drawbacks of poor eating habits and lack of exercise. He began to highly value his health, so this time he went home and was able to make diet and exercise changes quite effortlessly. In the process, he lost over thirty pounds and felt good.

Two years passed. Quite gradually, Jim had begun to slip back into his old ways of eating, drinking, and socializing. Once again, his body no longer could sustain his excessive ways, and he was rushed to the hospital for immediate quadruple bypass surgery.

This time, he really got it. He valued life as never before and changed his lifestyle and his choices, which were now congruent with his goals. It has been over ten years since then, and Jim has been living a healthy lifestyle. It took a wake-up call in the form of two near-death experiences before he was able to really see the value of a healthy lifestyle.

You don't have to wait for something "tragic" to happen before you can make lasting changes. The following exercise will help you to more effectively achieve greater congruency between your goals and your values.

Action

Step one

You can lower the status of a value that you are currently living but no longer want to be dominant. You'll need to show yourself why it needs to move lower on your list. Choose something that you are spending a lot of time doing, thinking about, and focusing on that you no longer want to have as a priority. List sixty drawbacks of having this value; they can be general drawbacks and specific drawbacks.

Do not minimize the importance of writing this down. Be creative and think outside the box. When you want to stop, take a break, but come back and write some more. You must keep finding drawbacks to what you are doing to the extent that you automatically place it lower on your value list.

Molly decided to choose her family obligations because she felt that it was so unfair that she did everything for her mom even though her other siblings were physically and financially able to help. They never offered to help, and she hated shouldering the burden of responsibility. She knew it was her fault for not speaking up, so maybe this exercise would help.

Drawbacks to doing everything for Mom and the family

It takes away from the free time I could be having for myself.
It makes me resent my mom and sisters.
It's not fair to me.
I hate myself because I don't speak up and feel like a coward.
It is causing me to hold grudges against my sisters.
It numbs me to the love for my mother that I know I have inside.
I do not get to do the things that are of high value to me.
I blame them for my life, even though I know it is my fault.
If I do not speak up, I will die with anger and resentment, and it's my loss.

It takes time away from the time I want to spend with Mackie.
Mackie and I argue about the amount I do for my mom and sisters.
Mackie could get tired of me and find someone else to spend time with.
Mackie could leave me and then I won't even have him as an excuse.
I have no time to even think about what I would love to do.
I have no time to contemplate changing what I am doing for my career.
I don't have the time to exercise.
This has caused me to put on twenty pounds over the past four years.
I end up eating fast, unhealthy food instead of good food.
Mackie used to rave about my nice figure, and now I look like a potato sack.

Molly kept writing and writing. Over one hundred drawbacks later, she burst into tears. She didn't realize how disempowered a life she was living and that she was harboring so much anger, guilt, resentment, and hatred. She knew that it was up to her to make changes, and now she could really see why it was so important. She didn't know how to make changes, but she knew it was time.

Step two

Now that you have lowered the status of a value that you no longer want to live by, select a value that you desire to elevate, but this time list the benefits. List both general and specific ways it will enhance your other high values and help you achieve your purpose. This action will move the value that you desire to a higher status.

Molly decided to choose free time for herself as the value she wanted to elevate. She found she could have made a never-ending list of benefits. She began to see why this was such a good exercise. She was already feeling a change within her. Within her heart, the sun began to shine with hope. She read on.

Personal Creed

We all have ways we would love to live. What guidelines and rules would you love to make decisions by and live your life by? Writing them out will give you something to read that can remind you of where you would like to play in your own game of life. Again, there is no right or wrong about it.

Action

Make a list of the guidelines for your life as you would like to live it now, and add to this list as you move through your life.

Molly looked up at the clock and could hardly believe that almost the whole day had gone by. Working on her values was definitely an enlightening experience. Pretty soon, it would be time to take a break for dinner, but before that, she decided she would write out a few personal creeds. It would be so good to have this to refer to.

Molly Malone
Personal Creeds

Live each day with an open mind and an open heart.
Affirm my purpose each day.
Express myself authentically.
Recognize and honor my intuition.
Trust that everything happens for a reason.
Recognize that my life is my responsibility.
Take only inspired action.
Release judgment and blame.
Make choices based on my inner voice.

Molly reread her list and realized that she had not been doing any of these things, but it still felt good to write them down and recognize that she had all of this within her. Her awareness of how far she had moved away from herself astounded her. She had been ignoring herself for so many years now and could only hope that she would be able to move herself into creating a purpose-filled and empowered life. So far, everything seemed like a faraway dream.

Your Specialness

As mentioned earlier, we are all spiritual beings connected on the soul level, but we are each unique as to how we express ourselves throughout our lifetime. You are not here on earth to be anyone other than your true self. What makes you the unique and special person you are? What makes you stand out? There is no "right" you or "wrong" you. You are *you*.

We are here on earth to be no one other than our true selves, despite what the ego tells us. There is no such thing as a "wrong" you because you are you. You are authentic.

You have an amazing combination of character traits, habits, interests, expertise, actions, and experiences that are exceptional and irreplaceable, ranging from the simple to the complex. When you can recognize all of who you are and what you have done, you will find your own unique expression. When you begin to capitalize on your uniqueness and value yourself for exactly who you are, others will begin to value you, as well.

You are unlike anyone else in this whole world, and that is what makes you special. Writing the answers to the questions at the end of this chapter will be valuable in helping you recognize how exceptional and irreplaceable you are.

When you find greater value within yourself, others will find greater value in you. You are one of a kind, and no one is able to compete with you.

Action

List the valuable combination of traits, actions, and experiences that are distinct, exceptional, and irreplaceable about you. They can be simple or elaborate. When you are finished, read through them and star the ones that most help you fulfill your mission or purpose.

It had been so long since Molly had thought of herself as unique or special. What was valuable about her? What had she done that made her stand out? "Nothing," she was tempted to say to herself, but she knew that was not the case. Twirling a strand of hair between her fingers, she started to look at the ways in which she was unique…

How am I special?

I was the first person in my company to land a ten-year contract with a major client and the first to receive a bonus and a pay raise without putting in a formal request.

I used my grandmother's recipe for beef stroganoff to raise over two thousand dollars for the senior center. It was the most successful fundraiser they have had to date.

I set up four different girlfriends on blind dates, and they are all in good relationships, now.

I can tie over one hundred different types of slipknots and have even made up a few of my own.

I am excellent at helping people make the right connections. I introduced my husband to his biggest client, found my client the perfect dog, recommended to my mother that she become a member of her now favorite book club, secured an investor for my friend's restaurant, and got major media coverage for Suzie's new beauty salon.

I can multitask in ways that no one can believe, and I am great at developing timesaving techniques for almost everything.

I have an ability to sell anything to anyone if I believe in it.

"Not bad," thought Molly, considering she hadn't expected to come up with anything interesting. She knew she could come back to this as her awareness about her uniqueness expanded.

Inspiring Moments

What were some of the most inspiring moments of your life? When and where did they happen? The moments I want you to recall are the ones that either brought tears to your eyes or brought forth a deep emotion that you felt in your heart. Whenever you experience an inspiring moment, it is actually your spirit whispering to you! You spirit is always trying to awaken you to inspiration so that you can feel the presence of balance and of spirit. These moments are moments of connection to your heart. Note them.

Action

Write down your three most inspiring moments. Every time you have an inspiring moment, be sure to add it to this list. When you can recognize and note moments that inspire you, you are more likely to allow inspiration to lead you. When you are living your life on purpose, you will experience many inspiring moments.

The only inspiring moments Molly could remember having in the last ten years happened today, as she was working on the exercises in this book and finding hope for her life for the first time. It was truly inspiring to realize that she had the power to shift things in her life – she just had to want to. Her life was not going to get better until she decided to do something about it, and she was inspired as never before.

Your Daily Affirmations

What you say to yourself has a great impact on your life and how you experience it. What are some things that you would love to say to yourself for your entire life? List them and read them daily. Creeds have to do with the way you live your life.

Affirmations are statements that are personally empowering to you. Some examples are:

Everything I desire is completely within my reach.
I do what I love and I love what I do, each and every day.
I attract financial opportunities each day.
I eat wholesome foods, a balanced diet, and nourish my body consistently.

Action

Write your affirmations in line with what you would like to create.

Molly was inspired to start, and once she started writing, she couldn't stop. There were so many things she wanted to affirm for her life.

My Affirmations

Today, I see new opportunities that enable me to live my purpose.

I make choices each day that honor me in new ways.

I learn something whenever I am with others.

I give myself permission to follow my heart.

I create my own happiness.

There is nothing I cannot do.

I have newly discovered values for my life, which I use to move forward in new ways.

I have social contacts that I can tap into to serve myself as well as others.

I adopt wise financial strategies in order to become debt-free.

I sleep at least seven to eight hours each night in order to function at my optimum.

I eat foods that nourish me.

I exercise and move my body and breathe deeply each day.

I take vitamins and honor my body.

I take the time I need for myself in order to find myself again.

I am filled with appreciation for my husband, my home, my work, my friends, and my family.

I follow a new path in life so that I can tap into a new source of inspiration.

"That should do it for now," thought Molly. She decided to print the list out and put it by her bed, along with her purpose statement, so she could read what she had written and inspire herself with her own words each morning when she woke up. She thought she would take a dinner break now and celebrate herself. She felt good about what she was doing and very productive.

She peeked ahead and saw that Chapter Four was about Clutter. "Ugh," she thought as she turned the page. She decided to see what it was about, and then she'd take a break.

Chapter Four
Alice's Feng Shui Basic Rule #1

Minimize Clutter

Where do I place a fountain to bring in more opportunities? Will hanging a crystal enhance my career? Should I paint my room green for better feng shui? These are frequently asked questions, yet small things like this will hardly make much of a difference, and even if they do, their effect will be short-lived. For the long-term, the foundation of your energetic environment will have a greater impact.

So where do you begin? We all know that for anything to last it must have a good foundation, and my experience has shown me certain basics that create a strong, energetic base. If you are willing to take some time and do the work involved in the basics, you will feel an enormous difference in the energetic atmosphere that your body and senses are exposed to in every moment.

Alice's Basic Rule #1: Minimize Clutter

When I mention clutter in presentations, some people sigh, others groan, and many nod knowingly. Most everyone relates to clutter, no one seems to like having it, and yet, unless someone is spring cleaning or a move is imminent, it's rare to get motivated to clear it out. If we are not consistent with our clutter clearing, we just seem to collect more and more of it as time goes on.

In addition, have you noticed how clutter seems to follow you everywhere? Your closet, garage, desk, purse, dresser, wallet, car… We all have so many things that we have certainly outgrown, no longer have a use for, and wouldn't miss, yet we still hold onto them.

Since everything in our environment is a reflection of what's going on in our inner environment, a cluttered home is directly correlated with the mental and emotional clutter we hold inside. Clutter is always a manifestation of what is going on inside the minds and emotions of the people who are living and working in the environment. Have you noticed how uncomfortable it is to live or work amidst other people's clutter? That is because you are feeling their "stuff."

The Energetic Representation of Clutter

The word *clutter* derives from the English word *clotter*, which means to coagulate. Clutter creates stagnant energy, and when energy stagnates, clutter accumulates, and vice versa. The more clutter you have, the more stagnant energy is attracted to you. Clutter slows down the flow of everything around it: the energy, the people, and the ability of the occupants to move forward. Clutter ties up our energy so that we have less of it available for use in moving our lives in the direction we desire.

Every part of your life is represented energetically in your environment; by clearing your clutter, you can transform a significant portion of your life. By sorting out your clutter, you sort out your life, which results in a release and renewal of your own life force. Clutter is really a hindrance in your life if you have a lot of it.

Why We Hold on to Clutter

Clutter is woven into our emotional energy. It ties us to the past instead of allowing us to live in the present moment, yet we hold on to it for various reasons. How many of these clutter scenarios do you relate to?

Clothes that don't fit

You have clothes in your closet that are a size or two too small for you (and they have been there for a very long time).

How many times have you looked into your closet and seen clothes that you used to wear when you were a different size (and secretly hope that one day you will be able to fit into again)? By keeping these items, not only do you constantly have a visual reminder that you are not where you once were, you keep yourself from accepting your current state.

Keeping outdated clothes binds you to the past. If you can accept where you are with your size in the present and let go of the clothes that represent the "old" you, you will have an opportunity to create a "new" you. Donating the clothes to a charity or similar place where they can be of use enhances the energetic benefit of letting them go.

Alice's Feng Shui Basic Rule #1

Expensive but unused items

You purchased an expensive item that you don't use and it just sits there, collecting dust.

Have you ever purchased something that cost "a lot" of money and not long after realized that it was not a wise purchase and in truth a waste of money? It may have been an exercise machine, a kitchen gadget, fancy software for your computer that you never found the time to learn, or a home improvement project that you meant to put together but never did.

Keeping these items (especially in plain view) constantly reminds you of your "mistake." Each time this item is in your view, you subconsciously judge yourself, which holds you in the past and makes it harder to move on. Sell, donate, or give away these items. There is great value in doing so. If you know that one day you will use the item, put it somewhere where you do not see it all the time.

Keeping things "just in case"

You keep a lot of things "just in case," and you have more things than you do space.

It is natural to want to keep things that you might need "someday," and as long as you have the space, doesn't it make sense to keep good, usable things for a rainy day? There is nothing wrong with keeping things, but look at the things you are keeping. Do you have five umbrellas but only two people living in the home? Do you have a whole closetful of shopping bags that you have saved after every excursion, some from many years ago? Do you have plates that you never use but take space in your cupboard?

Holding onto everything that comes into your possession shows an anxiety about the future and a lack of trust that the Universe will provide what you need exactly when you need it. When you open up space in your home or office, you open up the possibility that something new can arrive. Recycle usable things back out into the community.

Items from a past relationship

You have possessions from a break-up or a loss that happened a long time ago.

Getting rid of possessions after a break-up or a death is always difficult because it means that you really have to come to terms with your grief and loss. There is no set time when things "should" be cleared out, as it varies from situation to situation, but the sooner you are able to clear out possessions associated with a past relationship, the sooner you are able to live in the present moment, especially in the case of a break-up where there is no chance of being reunited. If you want to clear an ex-partner's energy out of your life, make sure that you do not store their items under your bed. Out of sight does not mean out of the range of influence.

Everything contains energy, whether it is the energy of the item itself (color, shape, essence) or the emotional energy associated with that person. Of course, it is fine to keep items to remember the positive aspects of a person's existence in your life. Clearing out others' things is for when you need to let go and move on.

A gift you are not fond of

You have a gift that someone gave you and you don't like it.

Have you ever received a gift from someone that just isn't "you?" What did you do with it? Display it or wear it anyway? Put it in the closet and bring it out only when the gift-giver is around? Or did you just let it become clutter in your environment?

A gift you don't like from someone you do like is one of the toughest things to deal with gracefully. Most people don't know exactly what is the right thing to do. What I always say is to honor the intent of the gift and be appreciative of the love that the person has for you and then donate it or give it away to someone who likes it and can use it. Feng shui-wise, it doesn't make sense to keep something that does not resonate with you.

Tied to Your Clutter?

Imagine that you are tied to everything in your environment by an invisible thread of energy. As such, you are literally tied to your clutter, even if you can't see it, because what is in your environment is energetically a part of you. Just think, you are dragging all your clutter around, no matter where you are or what you are doing, and you are losing your energy to it! This is a powerful image of how clutter weighs you down and why sometimes it seems so hard to move forward.

Remember the last time you cleared out your closet or another space in your home or office? It may have been when you organized, threw away, and donated items to a charity. How did that feel afterwards? Did you feel a lightness or renewed energy? When you clear out clutter, even a small portion of it, that energy is returned to you.

Clutter Defined

What constitutes clutter? This is what I consider clutter:

Things you don't use: this means anything in your home or office that you have no use for but are still storing. Old dining room chairs stacked up in the garage, the old dresser that you moved to the spare bedroom that is more in the way than anything, glasses in the back of your cupboard, etc.

Things you don't love: you know what these things are. If you have them just "because," then they don't serve a purpose or a need. If the glasses in the cupboard are a gift from your favorite auntie and make you feel warm and fuzzy when you see them, then keep them: they don't constitute clutter.

Things that are untidy or disorganized: an organized space helps facilitate an organized life. If things are piled up in plain view, or even if you have a very messy computer desktop, these are considered clutter because they detract energetically from ease and represent chaotic energy.

Too many things in too small a space: a way to look at it would be to make sure that everything in your environment has a "home." Just like you have a home, the keys should have a home, your shoes should have a home, and remote controls should have a home. Everything you own needs a space to call its own. If you live in a small apartment and this is not possible, then do the best you can to clear out what you can let go of and find "homes" for everything else. By doing so, you honor the items you have.

Anything unfinished: do you have projects that you "haven't gotten around to" because of lack of time or lack of interest or because they fall low on your priority list with everything else you have going on in your life? If so, don't forget that "unfinished things" take up space in your mind and zap your energy, as well. For example, have you ever said to yourself that you "should" clean the kitchen utility drawer? If you told yourself that, and you didn't do it, then every time you see that kitchen drawer, you are losing energy to the thought that you should clean the drawer. It is time to change your perception of what really "needs" to be done and what you can let go of.

P.S. The most frequently asked question I get about clutter is whether it still affects you even if it is not in plain view. The answer is yes. Even if it can't be seen, it still exists as a vibration that influences the energetic state of your environment. Being *out of* sight is better than being *in* sight, but it is still something you need to address.

Other Types of Clutter

So far, because we are talking about feng shui, I have only been referring to clutter in the environment. However, be aware that there are other forms of clutter that can zap your energy, such as schedule clutter, mind clutter, people clutter, food clutter, noise clutter, and car clutter…you get the picture!

Methods to Clear Clutter

There are several ways to approach the clearing of clutter. The best way will depend on what resonates with you and your personal clutter situation. Here are a few simple ways to get started.

Grand Master Lin Yun's theory of relativity

The theory of relativity states that whatever is closest to you affects you the most, so start clearing from where you spend the most time.

If it's your bed, then begin by clearing out under the bed and working on your nightstand so that you can wake up to a clean nightstand.

Next, what do you see when you open your eyes? Clear the clutter from that view and continue from there.

Alice's Feng Shui Basic Rule #1

If you spend a lot of time at a desk, that is a great place to start. As well, if you spend a lot of time in the car, then start by clearing out your trunk, glove compartment, and car seat pockets, and vacuum the interior.

The "Four-Corner" method: Stagnant energy accumulates in the corners

Mary Swick, known as "the feng shui lady" in Las Vegas, Nevada, shared with me a method that I have in turn shared with many of my clients. This method is excellent for quickly releasing energy back to everyone in your home and is helpful when you don't know where to start or lack the energy to get going.

Similar to how crumbs of food eventually end up in the grooves at the edge of a tile, so also does old stagnant energy end up at the edges of a room or home. The corners where the supporting walls meet are where most of the stagnant energy accumulates, and by clearing the corners first, you get the greatest energetic rate of return, which triggers a chain reaction of energy release back to you.

The way to start is to pick any corner in your home and clear it out. There could be nothing but a plant, and all you need to do is water and trim away dead leaves, or it could be a shelf where you have old magazines and books to sort through. Then go to the next corner and then the next. By the third corner, you will begin to feel a renewed sense of lightness and have more energy to embark on a full clutter-clearing journey. Once you finish the corners of the home, you can do the same thing in the corners of each room.

A simple idea to inspire change

Another idea to kick-start a path toward physical and sensory change is to choose a small area of your home (or office) that is lacking beauty, contains clutter, or is in plain sight and needs a boost. It could be a shelf, a small tabletop, a space on the floor, or any area that "calls" to you for enlightening. Even if there are many possibilities, just choose one and think of it as a fun project. Do anything and everything you can to make it beautiful, sacred, and filled with the expression of you. Seeing how something small can make a difference will help you gain inspiration and confidence.

Does It Ever End?

I have discovered that there is no such thing as an end to clearing clutter and no point of completion that you eventually reach. Being aware of clutter and clearing clutter in your environment is an on-going process that requires constant assessment and reassessment, just as our lives do.

It is important to remain constantly aware, as sometimes clutter sneakily takes over an area before you know it. If you are craving a new look in your home or environment and don't want to spend a lot of money, clear some clutter and move things around to see if that will give you the boost you need.

Molly allowed herself to really look at her home and assess her clutter. She knew she had a lot more things than she would like to admit and that there were certain areas of her home that she just "hated" because of all the disorganization, clutter, and mess. She had never before seen it as an energetic issue, but now she had a different perspective, and, amazingly (to her), she could actually "see" how her home really did mirror her life.

She had never seen any value in taking the time to get rid of things, but now she had a reason – and also a vision of how she would like to live. She decided that clearing out some of the accumulated clutter would be a benefit to her, and so she wrote it down in her feng shui notebook.

LIFEWORK

In the same way that we hold onto the past by keeping clutter in our environment, we hold on to clutter in our mental, emotional, and spiritual bodies in the form of resentment, guilt, regrets, blame, and faulty beliefs. The only difference between inner clutter and outer clutter is that inner clutter is invisible; however, both are similar in that they keep us from experiencing the fullness of life in the present moment.

Inner clutter is extremely draining. A part of your being must use its internal energy to hold on to the unnecessary things. As a result, you end up with heavy inner baggage that you lug around with you everywhere you go. In order to become more of the human "being" inside the human "doing," it is a good idea to take a look at the internal clutter you are holding on to.

Your Primary Beliefs

Since you were born, you have been forming countless beliefs in your mind. Some of them support you and are useful because they help you fulfill your goals and purpose in life. Other beliefs work against you. When you keep setting goals that are not in line with your higher values and your purpose, you eventually start to either believe that you can't achieve them or that they will be hard to achieve, and it will drag you down.

For example, let's say you have an inner belief that your house should be kept clean and orderly at all times. You may have gotten this from your mother, who kept her house immaculate for her own reasons. Now that you are an adult, you think that you, too, should be keeping your house clean, and because you don't, you judge yourself as "bad."

In this example, a clean house is actually of low value to you, and that is why it is hard to keep a clean house. If having a clean house is not high on your list of values, believing that you "should" goes against who you are. This belief doesn't support you.

In reality, there is no right and wrong about keeping a clean house. It is your belief and self-judgment that labels it as such. Someone else who loves and values keeping the home clean feels inspired to do it.

Action

Make a list of some of your beliefs. After you are finished, note with a star the ones that help you fulfill your purpose. Which beliefs do not help you fulfill your purpose? Reword them so that you can begin the process of consciously shifting your unsupportive beliefs into beliefs that support you. Remember, the only "right" is what is right for you.

For example, a primary belief that doesn't support you might be "I should spend time with family to show them that I love and care about them." Let's say your to-do list always has written on it, "spend time with family," yet every time you have the "time" to do so, other things draw your attention away, which causes you to feel guilty. By recognizing that there is no right and wrong about it, only what is right for you, you honor how you feel. You might reword this belief to say: "I show love and care for my family in many different ways" or "I love and care about my family even if I choose not to spend time with them frequently."

Do you have any of these common beliefs that likely take you away from your purpose?

- It's easier to sacrifice myself than have others blame me later for not helping them.
- It's up to me to make sure that everyone is happy.
- I have to do everything in order to get it done the way I want it.

Guilt and regrets

We hold on to guilt because we assume that something we have done in the past or something we are currently doing is creating more of a negative than a positive for us or someone else. Guilt is a heavy state of emotional conflict that we have all experienced at one time or another when we did or did not do something that we thought we should or should not have done. As a result, we internally bore a heavy responsibility for that "violation."

No matter whether it is self-imposed or imposed by others in the form of a "guilt trip," guilt is simply the result of an unbalanced perspective. Everything has two sides, and every thing, every action, every person, every circumstance, and every situation has both a benefit and a drawback. When you can see the benefits instead of only the drawbacks, you can dissipate the guilt you hold and release it from the inner clutter you carry.

Guilt seems to be caused by something that happened, but in reality, it is how you relate to what happened. What you are feeling guilty about is actually neutral—neither good nor bad. You are only judging it as bad, or others are judging it as bad, based upon a certain perspective and certain values, and you are holding on to it in the form of guilt. The truth is, we do not know enough to know the bigger picture, and holding on to guilt only serves to burden us unnecessarily. Fortunately, because you created the guilt, you can also release it.

Alice's Feng Shui Basic Rule #1

Action

List three things past or present that you feel guilty about. For each one, ask yourself the questions below and write down as many answers as you can think of. Your answers can be both general and specific. The more you write, the more you will bring to a state of balance and dissipate your lopsided perception of the guilt you are carrying. Doing this exercise will lessen the guilt you are carrying unnecessarily. Not only that, but if you keep working on finding more and more answers, you will eventually completely remove the weight of the guilt you are carrying.

Here are the questions to ask yourself about each of your guilts: How is what I feel guilty about a benefit or support to me or someone else, either past or present? What have I gained by doing or not doing what I am feeling guilty of?

Molly immediately knew she wanted to work on this one. In fact, she felt that what she was holding on to was so bad and so shameful that she had never told anyone before and didn't know how to let the guilt go. She saw it as the worst thing she had ever done.

About seven years into her marriage to Mackie, she had an affair with a co-worker for about eight months. Although the affair ended a few years ago, she had always felt like a horrible person because of it. Not a day went by that she didn't think of what she had done and feel a heavy sense of guilt. Molly had never thought to consider the positive aspects about what she did.

Because she had been thinking of this as a negative for so long, she took a long time to get started. She really couldn't think of anything positive, but finally she started to write…

GUILT BURDEN #1: *How has my affair with Roger benefitted me and/or Mackie? What have I gained from having this affair, both at the time and now, after the fact?*

- *I am less judgmental when I hear about other people's infidelities.*
- *I have a new viewpoint on what I need from Mackie.*
- *It has helped me to see what was missing in my relationship with Mackie and find words for it.*

- *I was able to enjoy a new style of affection, caressing, and intimacy.*
- *Roger helped me get through a challenging time at work when Mackie was not emotionally available to me because of his own work transitions.*
- *From Roger, I learned a lot about business and starting up a business.*
- *Meeting up with Roger gave me something to look forward to when things were glum.*
- *I found someone who could understand me in a different way than Mackie.*
- *When I could forget about feeling guilty, it was fun to get to know someone new intimately.*
- *The whole time I was with Roger, I didn't put the same demands on Mackie as I would have.*
- *Because of this, I believe Mackie and I made it through a time that could have been filled with arguments and blame.*
- *I learned about eating healthy because Roger was very much into eating well.*
- *I found out that "affairs" are not really "sordid," as I had always believed.*
- *No one ever found out, so Roger and I didn't have to go through any challenges because of our spouses' feeling betrayed.*
- *I realized after it was over that I did treasure Mackie more than I had thought.*
- *I started to see things in Mackie that I had taken for granted before.*
- *The relationship with Roger really enhanced my marriage with Mackie, though I never gave it credit before now.*

GUILT BURDEN #2: *On my father's death bed, as he was gasping for his last breath, he made me promise to take care of my mother. In the emotions of the moment, I promised. I have been doing so ever since, but I am now recognizing that Mom and my sisters have been taking advantage of this and that I want to let some of it go. Just the thought of letting go of some of that responsibility that I promised makes me feel guilty. The benefits?*

- *My mother will depend more on herself to do some of the things I currently do for her. This would be good for her brain activity and maybe contribute towards her longevity.*
- *If I say I am not available, my mother will have to call my sisters for help, and they will get a taste of what I have been dealing with.*

- *My sisters will get to spend more time getting to know Mom and who she is today.*
- *Mom will get to spend time with my sisters and with her grandkids.*
- *I will be healthier because I will be able to spend some time exercising.*
- *I will do less emotional eating.*
- *I will be more pleasant to be around.*
- *I will be more appreciated when I am available.*
- *I will be happier.*
- *I will have more time to do the things I am finding out I want to do for myself.*
- *I will not be resentful.*
- *I will be proud of myself for holding a new boundary and doing something that honors me, for a change.*

Molly reread what she had written. She knew she would have to come back to write more until she could convince herself to let go of her self-imposed guilt, but this was definitely a good start.

Resentment and blame

When we are filled with resentment, a part of us puts up walls of protection and closes down. We blame another for their action (or lack of action) and shut down, even though what we are experiencing is presenting itself so that we can grow. Think of a time when you once held resentment towards someone and how, in retrospect, you see it from a different perspective. Can you see how that experience helped you grow in some way? If not, you have not completely processed it and let it go.

It's hard to let go of resentment because we think it means:

- That we condone what we think is "wrong" behavior.
- That we have to let that person back into our lives.
- That continuing to feel hatred and resentment means we somehow have more control.
- That if we let it go and move on, we might get hurt again.
- That if we let it go and move on, the person won't get the punishment he or she deserves.
- That by holding on, we remain superior.

None of these is true. When you let go of resentment, you are not doing it for the benefit of the other person; you are doing it for you. Although it is natural to feel hurt initially, when you harbor imbalanced perspectives, it creates clutter in your being and holds you back from evolution and growth.

By taking the time to recognize that anyone you are holding resentment against is simply a reflection of a part of you that you have not acknowledged, you can begin to dissipate the resentment. As hard as it is to admit, or as impossible as it initially seems, if you can recognize the capacity in yourself to behave in the same way as the one who wronged you, you will free yourself to move on with your life.

Action

List any resentments you are actively holding on to, large or small, from the past or in the present. Some examples could be fairly small, such as: your spouse spends more time with his friends than you want him to, your wife has gained weight (and you married her when she was "slim," which was part of the attraction), your husband didn't fix the gate as he promised he would, your boss said that you could take off work and then, at the last minute, you couldn't get off so you had to cancel your plans, etc.

The resentment could come from something you perceive of as bigger: your best friend told another a secret she promised not to tell anyone, you found out your wife has been unfaithful to you with your brother, your sister borrowed money and never returned it and yet she was able to afford a new luxury car, etc.

Take each act of resentment and ask yourself when you have done something similar. The act was likely not in the same form, but if an action bothers you, it means that you have done it somewhere, at some time, or that you have it within you to do something similar. When you hold resentment towards another, put them down for what they have done, and judge their actions as wrong, looking within and realizing that you are not so different from them will help you neutralize the charge.

Going back to one of the examples above, these are some questions you could ask: If you resent your spouse for spending time with his buddies

Alice's Feng Shui Basic Rule #1

during free moments, where do you spend more time on things than your spouse would prefer? Or, perhaps more important, what are some things you love that you wish you allowed yourself to spend more time on? Maybe it's not about your husband spending time with his buddies but about you wanting to have his attitude about how to spend time and resenting him because you don't.

On the bigger issues, the larger your resentment, the more time you will need to spend on dissolving it. Look for any aspect of that kind of wrongdoing in yourself. You have to be very honest and work on this one with an open heart. If you are not able to find something in the past of the same magnitude, create circumstances in which you could see yourself possibly doing that which you are holding hurt and resentment for. The more you can relate to the action, the more you can neutralize the charge.

Chapter Five
Alice's Feng Shui Basic Rule #2

Have Things You Love Around You

Look around your home. What do you see — things that you love and cherish or items that are just there "because?" Often I have seen items on display in homes that I am curious about, and when I ask the occupant to tell me about an item, the response is, "Oh…my mother-in-law (who she can't stand) gave us that, and I really don't like it," or "I don't know. The landlord had it there when I moved in, so I kept it. It kind of spooks me out, though," (referring to an ethnic warrior mask).

Dr. David Hawkins, a renowned kinesiologist, states in his book, *Power vs. Force*, that "everything in your environment has a measurable vibratory frequency and energy that either supports you or weakens you." This can be understood in feng shui to mean that the figurine of your favorite animal that was given to you by your best friend, whom you really love, is an item that supports you, while the odd looking clock that is not your style and was given to you by a person who constantly bickers with you does not support you.

Remove What Doesn't Support You

Look to see what you have around you. Take away anything you do not absolutely love, and what you have left will support you energetically.

If there are things that you acquired during a time of loneliness, that energy of loneliness is still being "beamed" into your environment. If there is an item which is part of the "old you" and you have it just to have it, it would be a good energetic move to clear it out unless you love the memory it holds. Everything holds the energy of the time and space in which it was brought into your life. Keep this in mind when you are making a decision as to whether to keep something.

How an item holds energy

Some items in your environment can be considered neutral — such as a CD player. You may like its style, but basically, it is there to play music. Imagine that one day you and your spouse get into a heated argument about an issue that you just can't agree upon. You become emotional and, in turning your body, you bump a lamp that falls onto the CD player, leaving a gash on the face of it. That CD player still functions, but now it holds the emotional energy of that negative interaction.

Each time you put a CD in that player from this day forward, you are reminded (consciously or subconsciously) of that issue and the argument that ensued. That CD player is now no longer a neutral item. It is not supporting you in your environment, and it can energetically drain you.

What if my spouse and I disagree about an item?

When there are two or more people in a household, a difference of opinion often arises as to whether something is energetically supportive, especially an item in a common area.

Let's imagine the item in dispute is a funky wall hanging from a garage sale that you absolutely love and your spouse thinks is unsightly. How can you come to an agreement on this? One way is to reassign the meaning of the wall hanging to represent the love and respect you have for each other.

First, I would suggest rating the wall hanging on a scale of 1-10 as to how much you love it, 10 being the highest score. Then your spouse should rate the same wall hanging, but with 10 being highest amount of *dislike* for it. If you rate it a 9 and your spouse rates it a 7, then based on this rating, you love it more than your spouse dislikes it.

Next, I would ask your spouse if he or she loved you enough to allow that wall hanging to represent your love. If so, by agreeing to let it hang, your spouse has the opportunity to transform it from an "eyesore" into a gift of love because you like the wall hanging more than he dislikes it.

After such an exercise, the wall hanging takes on a new symbolic meaning, and each time you see it, you are grateful and see it as a gift. And every time your spouse sees it, it reminds him of how much he loves you and how important you are. The wall hanging has become a reminder of love instead of an instigator of disharmony. I have seen many couples use this process and find it effective.

Alice's Feng Shui Basic Rule #2

Gifts you do not like

If you receive something that you don't like, don't display it! We are always afraid that the gift giver is going to come back and say, "Hey! Where's that wooly mammoth statue I gave you?" However, that is no reason to put it in your environment if you know it doesn't support you.

Honor the intent of such a gift, feel the love behind the gift, be thankful, and then give it away or donate it. It is okay to do this. By not doing this, you neglect to honor yourself, the most important person in your life.

Molly could hardly believe the insight and awareness she was getting about her home. There were quite a few things in her home that she loved, like the hand-blown glass figurines of the lovebirds she bought when she visited Carmel with Mackie a few years ago and the end table she got at an artists' fair when they first got married. However, they were completely overshadowed by all the things she really didn't care for. As she looked around, she realized most of those things had been gifts or hand-me-downs from her mother, sisters, and friends.

Whenever someone offered her something they didn't want, she had trouble saying no, even if she didn't like the item. She just figured it was easier to take it and then get rid of it later, which she never did. It was even worse when someone gave her a present she didn't like. She felt obligated to display it in case they ever came over and asked her about it.

She thought long and hard about what types of things she loved and would like to have around her. She knew that she had always been attracted to fun, creative, one-of-a-kind artsy items, but sadly, when she looked around, she saw hardly anything remotely close to that. "Wow," thought Molly. Her home truly reflected where she was at. She could see that she had slowly but surely allowed others to take control of her life.

She picked up her pen and wrote in her notebook: "Donate everything I don't like."

LIFEWORK

In keeping with outer feng shui Basic Rule #2, only have things you love around you, which keeps your environment present with where you are now in your life, inner feng shui also delves into finding a new awareness of the present. Are you letting the past or perceived future dictate your actions?

Wouldn't it be wonderful to live without obligations and fears? It may not be humanly possible to let it all go, but it is possible to let go of a lot by being conscious of where you are holding yourself back. The more you bring to balance your perception of the past and the more you keep your mind free from fear of the future, the more inspired you can be in your present life.

Wisdom of an Ancient Philosopher

I heard a story originally told by the ancient philosopher Chuang-Tzu that is a good reminder of why it is so important to stay in the present moment.

A farmer in a small village had one horse, and it ran away. Since the village was so poor, his friends and neighbors came by to sympathize. "How horrible! How unfortunate it is that your horse has run away." The farmer replied, "Maybe."

The next day, the horse came home, and brought with him many wild horses. "Wow, how fortunate!" said the friends and neighbors. "Maybe," replied the farmer.

When the farmer's son was trying to tame one of the wild horses, he was bucked off and broke his leg. "How awful!" said the friends and neighbors. "Maybe," said the farmer.

Later, an army passed through the village, recruiting all able-bodied young men. The farmer's son was passed over because of his broken leg. "How lucky you are," the friends and neighbors said. You can guess what the farmer replied!

This story just demonstrates how, too often, we make judgments and see things from a certain perspective, which tends to keep us stuck in the past or lost in thoughts that create an unknown future filled with fear. If we can trust that life has two equal and complementary sides and find the balance, we can more easily stay in the present moment.

Alice's Feng Shui Basic Rule #2

What Keeps Us out of the Present Moment?

The Lifework for Basic Rule #2 involves looking at the past and what keeps you from experiencing the present moment authentically. We all have perceived obligations that hold us in an old pattern of doing things that are not in alignment with who we are now, in the present. You may believe that you "have to do" certain things, but it is quite useful to take a good look at what you are doing from a detached perspective.

Obligations

We all have things in our lives that we "should do" or "have to do" versus things we "want to do" or "love to do." The things we feel we "have to do" don't feel inspiring, yet we believe that it is our responsibility to do them. The more obligated we feel, the less inspired we are because we think that we have no choice. It's important to be clear about why you are doing what you are doing, otherwise you'll build up resentment for doing things you don't really want to do and feel guilty for not doing things that you think you "should do."

Can you think of some things that you have on your to-do list that are based on obligations, over-responsibility, guilt, fear of consequences, or remorse? If you don't make a change, these things will always be a part of your life and weigh you down.

Action

Make a list of things you do because you "have to," things that—if you had a "choice"—you would not have on your list of things to do. List anything and everything. Do not judge whether you should or should not be writing something down. Be truthful, and write down everything you are not inspired by and don't really want to do.

This is a further breaking down into actual reality of the details of your life that you don't enjoy. List the specifics of what you are spending your time, focus, money, and energy on that you no longer wish to place such a high value on.

This was easy, Molly thought. There were so many things she could write." Without skipping a beat, she began:

I would not:

- *Take my mother to every single one of her social appointments and doctor visits.*
- *Clean the house every week and do all laundry, bill paying, and grocery shopping.*
- *Give Susie a ride to her husband's office every Friday after work.*
- *Call my two sisters every day.*
- *Buy Christmas presents for all the family members and send out so many Christmas cards.*
- *Be in charge of the snack fund at work and be the one to replenish the snacks.*
- *Be in charge of the "Pick a Pork" Fundraiser each year for the homeless.*
- *Be on the "Greet your New Neighbor" board.*
- *Answer the door every time the doorbell rings.*
- *Go to lunch with Josie so often.*
- *Accept items from people just because they don't want them.*
- *Talk to Emma for so long and not every day.*

Wow! Molly hadn't realized there were so many things she felt obligated to do on a day-to-day basis. She would love it if she could get rid of even half these things. It just didn't seem possible; there were so many layers of complexity to it all, yet it did feel good to write it all down. She read on to the second part and did as was written.

Action

Look at each bullet point and write your answer in each case.

- Do you want to take this off your list?
- Is it necessary to knock this off your list? Yes | No | Why
- If you don't, how do you think you will feel two months from now? Four months from now? One year from now?
- If you do, how do you think you will feel two months from now? Four months from now? One year from now?
- If you *don't* let go of this, what are the drawbacks you will experience?
- If you *do* let go of this, what are the benefits you will experience?
- How is doing this a disservice to those who are benefitting?

- Is it time to let this go? If so, how do you plan to do it? Who do you need to talk to? How will you word this? Write your plan and pick a time to start.

Here are some examples of the drawbacks to holding on to obligations that you know you need to let go of:

- You risk physical, mental, and emotional exhaustion, which lead to physical ailments and diseases.
- You never attain personal peace with your life as it is.
- You don't get to do what you want to do.
- You will continue to be bogged down and will likely build resentment towards yourself and others.
- You will never be at rest and will always have these issues dragging on your emotions and energy.
- You could become so weighed down by your obligations that they are the only topic of conversation or focus of attention you have in your life.

Are these enough reasons? If what was once enjoyable no longer is, recognize also that you are not who you were back then and focus on the fact that, as difficult as it is, it is time to redefine. Remember, if you died tomorrow, someone else would step up to the plate to fill that void. You have to be the one to let go first.

If you just cannot let an obligation go, change your perception. Perception is in your mind and in your control. In this case, write forty reasons on how you can gain by doing this. How are you benefitting? The more you can see a benefit to yourself for what you are doing, the less of a drag this obligation will feel.

Fear

Basic Rule #2 also places an importance on addressing our fears about the future and dissipating them so that we are able to live in the present. Fears are assumptions we make about the future in which we envision it to be more negative than positive. By taking the time to see that no matter what might happen in the future there will be a benefit, we can more easily begin to trust in the present moment as it unfolds.

It is natural for human beings to experience fear, and at some times more than others. We think that if what we fear were to happen, it would bring us pain, challenges, and suffering or stand in the way of a future ideal. Sometimes what we experience as a big fear is just a collection of smaller fears that constantly play in our mind. Sometimes we fear that our current challenging circumstances will continue on into the future. Fears can also be based on nothing tangible at all and have no basis in reality yet still feel very real. No matter what the fears are, they keep us from experiencing the present moment.

A perfect example of ungrounded fear is the story of my aunt. She has been married to my uncle for sixty-eight years now. Her biggest fear was that my uncle would leave her for another woman, and she worried about it incessantly throughout her whole life. She constantly told anyone she was talking to that she was afraid of the day that my uncle would leave her for some "floozy." My uncle is now ninety-five years old, and they are still together although she has developed Alzheimer's. For the past few years, she has been in a care home, yet he continues to visit her daily, even though she does not recognize him. He shared with me that in their all their years together, he has never once considered leaving.

It's ironic, isn't it? We want to be happy and at peace, yet fear causes us to be anxious in the present and worry about the future. Our internal dialogue keeps us trapped. It takes what we have seen or experienced in the past and projects it into an imaginary, scary future. And as long as our attention is jumping from the past to the future, we have no opportunity to experience things as they truly are in the present.

Dr. John Demartini has a great definition of fear. He says, "fear is an assumption that in the future you will experience through your senses or through your imagination more pain than pleasure, more negative than positive, and more loss than gain." Everything that happens in our lives has two equally balanced sides to it, and to have true peace and fulfillment, we must recognize both sides in order to open ourselves to peace. No matter

Alice's Feng Shui Basic Rule #2

what we experience, there is an equal balance of support and challenge, and if we are not seeing it, we are viewing life from a skewed perspective.

To balance our fears, we must ask ourselves balancing questions and stop living in an elusive search for a one-sided life experience of only pleasure and gain. If we fear the pain and fail to recognize how the pain will benefit us, we cannot live in the present. We can choose to be victims of our past and live in a projected fear of the future, or we can choose to be masters of our destiny by embracing both sides of the coin of life.

Action

Write out your fears, both significant and seemingly insignificant. Going back through your list, do the following exercise so that you can let go of each fear:

- List 30-40 general and specific *benefits* that you would experience should this fear manifest.
- List 30-40 general and specific *benefits* that others would experience should this fear manifest.

When you take the time to actually write out your answers, you increase the effectiveness of bringing the imagined fear into balance so that you can live more in the present moment. There is *always* a benefit for everything you experience in your life. The more benefits you can find, the more balanced you will feel.

Chapter Six
Alice's Feng Shui Basic Rule #3

Pay Attention to the Pictures on the Wall

The pictures in your environment, like the pictures you hold in your mind in the form of visions and goals, affect you more than you may realize. The pictures on your wall are constantly "speaking" to you by projecting the energy of what they are depicting into your environment. This energetic message is continuously being picked up by your subconscious and sent to your brain as you spend time in that environment. Look around you. What are your pictures saying to you? What visions are you projecting?

Do you have pictures that depict desolation, emptiness, loneliness, turbulence, and fatigue, or do you have images that speak of life force, abundance, vitality, peace, possibilities, and harmony?

Mary Swick, in an article that is now found in her e-book, *Life-Changing Feng Shui*, was the first to bring to my attention the importance of the messages sent by the pictures we place in our environment. After awakening to this concept, I became very conscious of artwork as I consulted on people's homes and businesses. I have found hundreds of amazing correlations between what was going on in people's lives and what I saw on their walls.

Pictures: A Consultation Story

The first consultation I did after becoming aware of the importance of artwork is the best and most memorable. A man his mid-forties who had been divorced for seven years thought perhaps feng shui could help him find a relationship, the one thing he felt was lacking in his life.

Upon entering his home, I noticed that the space was warm and inviting for a bachelor. I could see his attention to detail, and the place had a feeling of comfort. We sat down to talk. All was well in his life, except that he had no relationship. He stated that he had minimal opportunities to meet women, and those he did meet seemed to "take off," sometimes for other men and sometimes for other cities.

Observation of the space

In feng shui, the bedroom represents relationships and so, of course, this was where I had anticipated that we would do most of our work.

Even knowing this, I was surprised by the room after observing the rest of the home. The bedroom contained no plants, no decorative figurines, no warm and inviting colors, and no carpet. Most interesting to me, however, were the two pictures on the wall.

Pictures tell a story

The first picture, placed directly over his bed, was a large, poster-sized black and white aerial photo of dried, cracked lava flow. It looked desolate and grey and lacked any feeling of life. On the other wall, one that he could see while lying in bed, was a picture of an airplane taking off.

The two pictures related specifically to what he was saying to me in his living room: he had a lack of women in his life (black-and-white photo of lava), and the women he did meet seemed to "take off" (airplane taking off)!

The chicken or the egg

Now, did the pictures cause the circumstances or did the circumstances cause him to display those particular pictures? What do you think? What we choose to place on the outside is simply a reflection of what is happening on the inside.

If, in an unaware state, you hang a picture without really looking at its message or its energy, and if it happens to resonate with something you do not want to continue in your life, then you will continue to subtly have your thinking reinforced through those images.

If, in an aware state, you place images of something you would like to create in your life, you will be assisting yourself energetically to see the possibilities of bringing that forth. When I asked him why he had hung those two particular pictures in his bedroom, he said there was no specific reason. At the time, he had not really thought about it except that they seemed to fit in the bedroom.

Alice's Feng Shui Basic Rule #3

I suggested that he display pictures that represent relationship energy, such as items shown in pairs and images depicting vibrancy, life force, abundance, and love. I also invited him to consider putting time into his bedroom to make it as warm and welcoming as the rest of his home.

Use Your Walls for Energetic Support

Take a look at the images on your walls. If the images remind you of a time from which you want to move forward, or if they do not emit the kind of energy you want to surround yourself in, then it is time to change. Choose pictures that have inspiring messages. When in doubt, nature, landscapes, happiness, vitality, and favorite places and items are a great place to start. Commit to using your walls not just as structural support, but as energetic support, as well!

Your walls are an excellent place to focus on when you want to bring positive energy into your life and emphasize visions of what you want to create. It's important to understand that, energetically, even if you are not looking at something, what is around you constantly streams its energy into your subconscious. We create our lives both consciously and subconsciously, so make sure that the "messages" on your walls are what you want to "hear."

Molly looked at her pictures. At first, she couldn't even remember why she had placed those particular pictures on the wall. All at once, she remembered. They were the pictures from when they had bought the house! They had bought the model home, and it had come with the pictures, so they just kept the art up, thinking that one day they would change it.

All the pictures were quite abstract and not very inspiring, at all. They were the same style throughout the house, just in different shades and shapes. Looking closely at the ones in the living room now, not only were they dusty and crooked, they were kind of depressing, with a lot of grey and brown tones.

"New artwork!" wrote Molly in her feng shui notebook.

LIFEWORK

Just as you can choose to place pictures on your wall that project positive visions for your life, you can choose to set goals that are in line with the visions that you see for yourself.

It is similar to having a destination in mind when you get in your car to go somewhere, even though there may be several different ways to get there. Goal setting is no different. When you take the time to plan your life journey, you are more likely to end up where you would like to go.

Many Find Goal Setting a Turn-Off

Many people are turned off by goal setting or have given up on it because, in the past, they set goals and often failed to achieve them. Setting goals can be tricky and work against us when we don't know how to go about it. However, goals are an extremely important component of living your purpose, so it is valuable to learn how to set them.

You have already seen from previous lifework and examples that, if you set goals that are not in line with what is truly important to you, you will not be able to reach those goals. Remember Jim, the man I mentioned in Chapter Three, who had two heart surgeries as part of his challenging journey towards better health? Also, if you set goals that are unrealistic, you will only experience frustration and feelings of failure, since such goals will be virtually impossible to attain.

What are goals?

You can't just dream about something and then hope that it happens. If you really want something in your life, you must set tangible goals in order to achieve it. I like to think of goals as destination points along the path of life. I read about a study that showed that only three percent of the population consciously sets any goals, and that these three percent accomplish more than the other ninety-seven percent combined. So, if you want to accomplish something meaningful in your life, then setting goals is mandatory.

Alice's Feng Shui Basic Rule #3

How to set goals

The goals you set must be realistic, possible, and measurable. If you set goals that are aligned with your purpose, you have a high likelihood of achieving them. If not, you will procrastinate in doing them and end up frustrated. You must have an action plan for your goals so that you have a strategy by which to achieve them.

Do not get overly excited and set goals that are greater than your true capacity, because that will only set you up for failure and frustration. On the other hand, if you set goals that are too easy for you, you will get bored and lose out on opportunities to grow.

The best way to set goals for yourself is to stay centered in your heart and set true, reasonable, and inspiring goals. In this way, you will continually inspire yourself and accomplish great things.

Think about your life

Take some time to think about some things that you would like to be doing in your life as time goes on, and write down some of your ambitions. What are some benchmarks for your life? Imagine where you would like to be. For this next portion, don't worry about how you are going to get there, just ask yourself a few questions and see what is true for you.

Action

Ask yourself the following questions and take some time to write down the answers.

- What would you love to be doing in one year's time?
- What would you love to be doing in five years?
- What would you love to be doing in ten years?
- What about twenty years?
- More than twenty years?

Food for thought

We are all here on earth for a limited and unknown amount of time. We never know at what point our life on earth will be over. No astrologer, no psychic, and no one alive that I know of is able to predict when this day will come. Do you feel that you are doing everything you can with the talents that you have developed or with the gifts that are uniquely yours? Are you living the life that you would love to be remembered for? What are some things that you have yet to fulfill?

Action

Write the answers to the following question:

What are some things you would love to fulfill in your life?

Molly realized that she had never asked herself this question in her whole life. This would take some time to really get clear on, but three things immediately came to mind:

- *I would love to make a difference in people's lives.*
- *I would love to have a business that serves others.*
- *I would love to be my own boss.*

A Look at Death

Paulo Coelho said in *The Alchemist*, "We are all walking towards death, but we never know when death will touch us and it is our duty, therefore to look around us, to be grateful for each minute. But we should also be grateful to death because it makes us think about the importance of each decision we take, or fail to take, it makes us stop doing anything that keeps us stuck in the category of the 'living dead' and, instead, urges us to risk everything to bet everything on those things we always dreamed of doing, because whether we like it or not, the angel of death is waiting for us."

Action

We only have a certain time on earth. Think about how you would love to be remembered. Write what you would love to be remembered for.

Molly thought about it and wrote:

I would love to be remembered as someone whose life inspired others. I would love to be remembered as someone who used their talents to help others. Finally, I would love to be remembered as a person who was happy and at peace with her life in hopes that it would help others seek the same.

Alice's Feng Shui Basic Rule #3

Setting a Goal

Look back to see what you wrote for what you would love to be doing in one year's time and pick something that you would love to accomplish. Remember, a goal is not your purpose, but it is a point along the way that is in line with your purpose. You know you have picked the right goal because, when you envision it, you will feel uncomfortable and also see it as a bit scary and challenging, all at the same time. By actually working on this goal, you will feel stretched beyond your comfort zone and forced to grow in new ways.

Action

Write down that one goal and ask yourself the following questions. Be sure to write out the answers so that you will have a reference point.

- Why do you want to achieve this goal?
- What do you feel is standing in the way of achieving this goal? List the obstacles or problems that you see.
- How do you plan to dissolve these obstacles or issues in advance? When will you do it?

Wayne Dyer, renowned writer and speaker, always says, "When you change the way you look at things, the things you look at change." When you apply this line of thought to your problems or your perceived obstacles, your perspective begins to change. Everything you take a look at from a higher vantage point (as you are doing here) contains the seed of an opportunity for a solution.

- What is the first thing you will do to achieve this goal? When will you do it? Write it on your calendar.
- What are the next three things you will do to achieve it?
- What are the next three things you will do to achieve it after that?
- Who can you ask to hold you accountable? Write down the person's name so you can call and let them know.
- Look at your life purpose once again and write down how reaching this goal will help you fulfill your life purpose.
- What positive things do you envision you will gain by achieving this goal?

- What challenges do you envision you will experience once you achieve this goal?
- How will you reward yourself once you have achieved this goal?

Molly had a flash of insight as she was reading! She realized there was something she really wanted to do in life. There was something she totally loved, and after thinking about it, she began to see that she could actually make a business out of it – her love of matchmaking!

It made total sense for her. She was always bringing people together from the diverse network of those she knew, and it had resulted in quite a few weddings over the years. And the couples were still married and even sent her cards on their anniversaries. People always came to her to see if she knew anyone for them. She enjoyed setting up singles' dinners and having people meet in a safe place. She always had a sense about people, and she loved the process of connecting them.

Molly spent the next few hours working on the strategy she would use to reach her goal, which was to begin mapping the way towards her own business: Molly's Matchmaking Magic.

She could hardly wait to begin. She knew in her heart that this would help her to fulfill her purpose.

Chapter Seven
Yin-Yang and the Five Elements

Natural Balance and the Flow of Energy

Many Eastern and Western philosophies, as well as science, tell us that the universe is composed of two complementary, opposite qualities that are expressed at all times. In feng shui, these qualities are known as *yin* and *yang*. Yin symbolizes the passive side of nature, and yang represents the active side. Think night and day, sun and moon, or a rushing river versus a still lake.

We experience the yin and yang of complementary opposites in every moment of life, internally and externally, through all of our senses and in all four of our bodies (physical, emotional, mental, spiritual). We experience it in the form of light and dark, hot and cold, left and right, happy and sad, pain and pleasure, positive and negative, and support and challenge, to name a few complementary opposites.

Tai Chi Symbol

The Tai Chi Symbol

You may have seen the black and white symbol at the beginning of this chapter before. It is called the Tai Chi symbol or Yin-Yang symbol and is always associated with feng shui. It represents the energy relationship between yin and yang and is one of the core philosophical principles upon which feng shui is based. Through these two elements, it represents the entire universe and all phenomena.

In this symbol, the elements of yin and yang are depicted as inseparable, for within yin there is yang, and within yang there is yin, one seamlessly leading into and out of the other. The opposites are viewed as one entity; they co-exist in a state of balanced harmony, as shown in the symbol. Nature is the perfect model of the balance of yin and yang. Our four bodies (physical, emotional, mental, spiritual), when in the ultimate state of balance, exist in a perfect dynamic of yin and yang.

Yin/Yang in Outer Feng Shui

We use the yin/yang principle in outer feng shui when we strive to balance the opposites in the environment so as to create a harmonious energy appropriate for the intended activity. For example, a bedroom that is too yang (bright, hot, and noisy) does not support quality sleep, whereas an office that is too yin (dim, cool, and passive) could cause one to feel relaxed to the point of unproductivity.

To balance these spaces and best serve their purposes, we could add yin-enhancing elements to the bedroom, such as thicker shades and a cooling air-circulating system, and yang elements to the office, such as brighter lighting and stimulating artwork.

Events can be identified by their natural yin or yang focus, as well. For example, funerals are considered the ultimate of yin energy and dance parties are the extreme of yang energy. Hip-hop music at a funeral would be as obviously out of balance as meditation music at a punk rockers' dance club.

The Yin/Yang Balance in Your Environment

Take some time to look at each room in your house through your "yin/yang eyes." Is the space appropriately balanced for its purpose? Generally, the more public and active the area's function, the more yang it needs to be, and the more private the area, the more yin.

Ask yourself questions as you go through your home. Is the dining room appropriately lit? Does it look like a dining room, or are there things in it that are not related to food, health, and eating? Is your bedroom truly a place of rest, or do you have a lot of work and stress reminders in the bedroom? I often see ironing boards, laundry, office items, and bills in the bedroom. These items represent yang energy, which is contrary to the yin energy of rest that is appropriate for the bedroom.

Yin/Yang in Inner Feng Shui

Yin and yang can also describe our emotions and can be used as a guide when working with our inner feng shui. For example, a man who is overly yang would tend to be more impatient and easily angered than most. His yang energy could be tempered by living in a more calming environment. On a personal level, he would likely be attracted to someone who was his complementary opposite: patient, quiet, and peaceful. What we don't have within, we seek without in order to bring ourselves a sense of balance and wholeness.

As another example, a woman who is in a very yin state could appear to be withdrawn, passive, and shy. She would benefit by being in a yang environment, surrounded by people who are optimistic and positive. She would likely be attracted to someone who is vibrant and upbeat.

Yin and Yang Traits

Yin and yang can also relate to common human traits. Traits such as introverted or extroverted, quiet or loud, aggressive or shy, daring or timid, nice and mean, or greedy and generous all exist in various forms within us, and we express one or the other depending on the circumstances or situations we are in.

We like to think that we have certain traits and not others, and we judge the ones we recognize in ourselves as either "good" or "bad," when in fact they are neither. Each of us has all the traits within us, and recognizing this is key to balance.

Traits we admire

When we admire a trait in another, it's because we don't see the same trait in ourselves. We see the trait as outside ourselves, yet interestingly, any trait that we see in another we do actually have within ourselves. When we can find where that trait exists in ourselves, we bring forth a state of balance within.

For example, you may admire someone who gives large sums of money to help people in need and think of them as amazingly generous. You may put them up on a pedestal and place yourself below them because you perceive that you don't give as much as they do.

In this case, you would look for generosity within yourself in a different form. Where have you helped others and given generously of your time, advice, or energy? Where have you had an impact on someone's life? Try to see that you are just as generous as the person you admire, but your generosity comes in a different form.

You may say, "Well, that's not the same, because he gives so much money." Money is actually just one of the forms of energy exchange; you see it as different simply because you haven't realized the value of your generosity in the form of time, love, and focus and the impact it has had on others. Until you can see that what another person does is no different from what you do, just presented in a different form, your perspective will remain unbalanced.

Traits we abhor

In the same way that we admire in others a trait that we don't think we have, when we see a trait in others that we abhor, we also have that within us; we just don't recognize the form it takes. The trait that we abhor is brought to our attention so that we can see and accept it as something we have within ourselves but have not acknowledged.

For example, you may really hate it when you go to a store and the salesperson is rude, talks down to you, or ignores you by serving another customer before you, even though you were there first. You are irritated and think, "I would *never* be rude like that. I am always nice to others."

Be open for a moment and ask yourself this: who do you look down on and want to treat like the salesperson treated you, even if you have not done so? Whatever you suppress, others will express. Or maybe you can see that there have been times when you have treated yourself that way. Where do you refuse to give yourself the time of day? Where do you fail to value your time and energy? Where have you put yourself last?

Yin-Yang and the Five Elements

Everything we experience is designed to bring us into a state of a balance. In reality, you have that rude trait within you. As long as you don't acknowledge rudeness as a part of you, others' rudeness will really bother you. Once you own it, it pairs up with its complementary opposite trait of niceness (which you know you have) and balances out. Once this happens, rude salespeople in the future will not irritate you to the same extent.

The Five Elements

The yin/yang theory of complementary opposites that I just shared is a very important foundational concept used in feng shui to bring balance to an environment. There is another system I'd like to introduce you to. It's the five element system, and it will lead you towards a deeper understanding of feng shui, balance, and energy movement. The five elements can be applied to both inner and outer feng shui.

According to this theory, everything in the world can be divided into the qualities of the five elements that are found in nature: water, wood, fire, earth, and metal. The elements themselves, or their representations in the form of colors and shapes, can be used to balance an environment.

In outer feng shui, the five element theory is used to determine which element is dominant or deficient in a space and, from there, positive energetic adjustments are made to balance the area. In inner feng shui, we can use the traits that are represented by the elements to bring balance and awareness to ourselves in the same way that we can with the complementary, opposite yin and yang traits.

Each element is a form of energy with its own unique qualities and connection to the world of nature. Each element also has a corresponding shape, a season, a taste, a direction, an organ, a psychological characteristic, a color, (and more). In the following section, I will define each element and give you the most useful correlations so that you can assess and then easily bring elemental balance to your environment. Yin and yang examples of each element are included to show you how you can add yin or yang elementary energy as needed.

Wood

Quality: Growth
Color: Green, blue
Shape: Columnar, rectangular
Physical Representations: Living trees and plants
Yin Wood: Dead plants, driftwood, potpourri
Yang Wood: Green healthy plants, live flowers

Wood represents traits such as new beginnings, growth, generosity, strength, vitality, flexibility, and creativity. The wood element can be seen in trees, plants, and flowers. It is symbolized by tall columns, which mimic the shape of trees. Tall buildings and skyscrapers represent the wood element and show growth in a city. Wood represents energy that moves vertically.

Too much wood can make you feel overwhelmed, rigid, stubborn, or inflexible. Too little wood can manifest as stagnation, lack of ambition, or lack of creativity.

People who have "wood personalities" are active and always on the go. They are assertive and direct and have a lot of ambition. They usually love nature and have a lot of trees or plants in their environment.

Ideas for adding the wood element to a space:

- Fresh plants or real-looking silk plants
- Natural fabrics and fibers such as cotton
- Wood furniture
- Things that are green or blue
- Striped items or columnar items
- Nature-inspired themes and designs, such as landscapes and florals

Fire

Quality: Expansion
Color: Red
Shape: Triangle, pyramid

Yin-Yang and the Five Elements

Physical Representations: Candles, lights, fireplace
Yin Fire: Candles, incense, soft lighting
Yang Fire: Fireplaces

Fire represents traits such as expressiveness, inspiration, attention, transformation, boldness, activity, energetic intensity, and brightness. The fire element can be seen in features such as fireplaces, barbecues, and stoves, as well as in angular designs with sharp edges and points. The pointed Transamerica pyramid-shaped skyscraper building in San Francisco represents the fire element. This fire shape has gotten so much attention that it defines the skyline of the city.

Too much fire in an environment can trigger anger, aggression, irritability, and impulsive behavior. Too little fire, on the other hand, can manifest as emotional distance and low self-esteem.

People who have "fire personalities" are captivating and bold. They love attention and are charming and easily excitable. They are usually fun to be around and are frequently seen as the life of a party.

Ideas for adding the fire element to a space:

- Candles, sunlight, and incandescent lights
- Animal prints, fur, and silky fabrics
- Anything in shades of red, purple, or other fiery colors
- Objects with points and angles
- Things that resemble diamonds or sunbursts
- Art that includes people and animals

Earth

Quality: Stability
Color: Yellow, earth tones
Shape: Squares, cubes
Physical Representations: Pottery
Yin Earth: Moist soil
Yang Earth: Dry hardened earth

Earth represents traits such as physical strength, order, stability, reliability, patience, balance, grounding, and nurturing. The earth element can be seen in anything made from stone, brick, ceramics, tile, and terra cotta. Buildings that are made of the earth element are low to the ground and are long lasting, the essence of stability.

Too much earth will make a space feel heavy, and inhabitants will experience boredom, laziness, or sluggishness. Too little earth and people feel ungrounded, flighty, and disorganized.

People who have "earth personalities" are warm and kind-hearted and look huggable. They like to collect things and have many knickknacks around the house. They love to nurture others and are always around when you need them. They are willing to commit to jobs or relationships for the long term.

Ideas for adding the earth element to a space:

- Items that are square, cubed, or rectangular
- Low surfaces
- Landscape images
- Pottery, tile, and earth-derived objects
- The colors of earth
- Heavy, solid-looking items

Metal

Quality: Contraction and intelligence
Color: White, metallic shades and pastels
Shape: Round, spherical
Physical Representations: Metal sculptures or objects, gold or silver
Yin Metal: Soft and pliable silver or gold
Yang Metal: Hard metals, such as steel

Metal represents traits such as clarity, logic, organization, perfection, focus, success, communication, detail, righteousness, refined tastes, elevated style, and intelligence. The metal element can be seen in buildings that have domed roofs and curved walls. Buildings with a lot of glass are also considered metal because of their reflective qualities.

Too much metal in your surroundings will cause you to be critical, overly chatty, and to speak without thinking things through. When there is not enough metal in the environment, it manifests as a feeling of cautiousness, reserve, and blurred focus.

People who have "metal personalities" love minimalism. They like blank walls and monochromatic color schemes. They are thinkers and perfectionists, and are organized, clean, and live either very simply or very nobly. They will give away things easily because they do not like to accumulate clutter.

Ideas for adding the metal element to a space:

- Anything made of metal or in metallic colors, such as silver, gold, or bronze
- White, silver, or light pastels added to the color scheme
- Round, domed objects in plain view
- Organizational elements that create order

Water

Quality: Stillness and renewal
Color: Black, dark blue
Shape: Undulating, wavy, flowing
Physical Representations: Fountain, aquarium, pond
Yin Water: Still water, paintings of water
Yang Water: Fountains and fish tanks

Water represents traits such as wisdom, spirituality, flow, stillness, travel, communication, influence, calm, maximum concentration, and rest. Water is present in the view of the ocean, a lake, a river, or a swimming pool. Water has no definite shape, so buildings that have an amorphous shape, like the Guggenheim Museum, are considered water-shaped structures.

Too much water in your environment can stimulate an extreme of emotions and increase the sense of being off-balance. It can make you feel overwhelmed, as if "drowning" in problems. Setting boundaries with others is difficult with an excess of water. With a lack of water, the inhabitants may feel lonely, isolated, and stressed and feel that there is no way out.

People who have "water personalities" like to live near water, take long baths, or have images of water around them. They love to meditate, tend to "go with the flow," and enjoy experiences that take them deep within themselves. They may be considered offbeat and quiet to those who don't know them well. They are unique individuals.

Ideas for adding the water element to a space:

- Black, navy blue, or other deep, saturated tones
- Mirrors, which represent water
- Water features, such as fountains or aquariums
- Images of bodies of water found in nature
- Objects or fabric that flows and drapes well
- A still place of beauty

The Five Elements

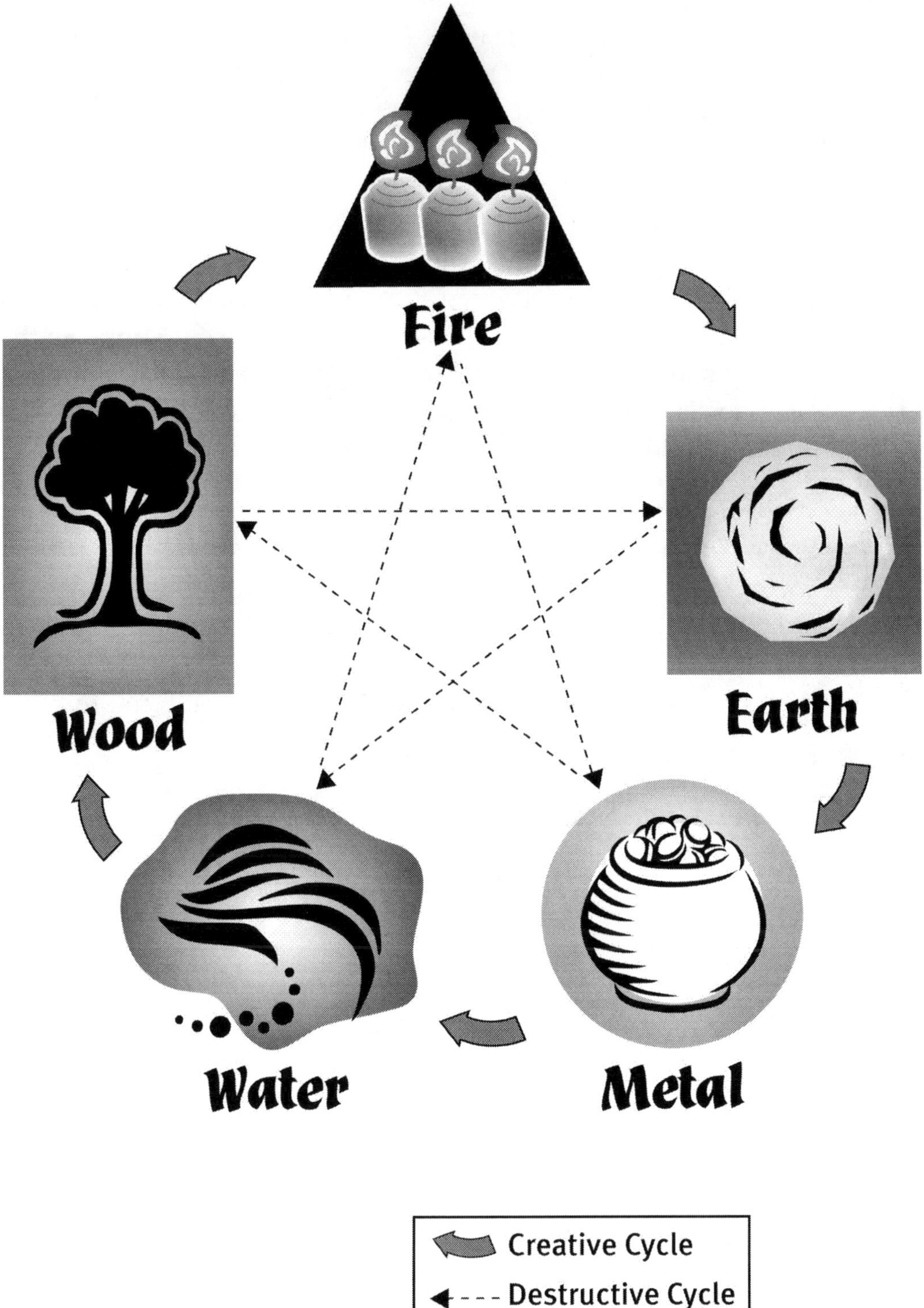

Cycles of the Five Elements

The five elements theory has the same underlying philosophy as the yin/yang theory: that of constant change, evolution, and seeking balance. The five elements of wood, fire, earth, metal, and water are in continuous movement in nature; they operate and interact in "creative" and "destructive" cycles to maintain balance. Understanding these cycles is very simple and can be useful in creating an elementally balanced environment. It is quite amazing how the elements relate to each other!

The Creative Cycle of the Elements

To explain the creative cycle, (also known as *the generative cycle*) the elements are placed in a circle in a specific order, where each element supports the elements on either side of it. Think of it as phases of a constantly moving, never-ending cycle. Each element leads to another in the same way that day turns into night or the seasons progress.

- Wood feeds Fire (the fuel for fire is wood)
- Fire creates Earth (ashes from a fire replenish earth)
- Earth births Metal (gold and ore are mined from the earth)
- Metal transforms to Water (when metal is heated, it changes to liquid)
- Water nourishes Wood (trees and plants need water to grow)

The Destructive Cycle of the Elements

Despite the name, the destructive cycle is not "negative" or "bad." It is simply a way to describe how the elements cyclically consume each other, versus how they support each other. This cycle is sometimes referred to as the *transformative cycle*.

- Water puts out Fire (fire is extinguished by water)
- Fire melts Metal (metal is burned by fire)
- Metal chops Wood (wood can be cut with an axe)
- Wood depletes Earth (earth is penetrated by growing trees)
- Earth dams Water (water is absorbed by earth)

How to Use the Elements in Outer Feng Shui

The creative and destructive cycles clearly show how natural forces interact. When the elements in your environment are in equilibrium, you sense more peace and harmony. When they are in conflict or out of balance, you may experience more obstacles.

When applying the elements to your environment, you can use the physical representation, the corresponding color, or the correlating shape. Be creative and have fun! Don't be concerned about whether what you want to do is "right." Use the elements and their cycles described here as basic guidelines and tune into your intuition. Remember, if it feels good, then it is right for you.

Elemental Use: Method Number One

Use all the elements together

Use all the elements together in a space to add power, movement, and balance and to create an atmosphere of wholeness. Do this in a small area, in a particular room, or a specific place of focus.

For example, to elementally balance your bedroom: If your carpet is beige (Earth) and your walls and dressers are light (Metal), you could choose a bedspread with warm colors (Fire), add sage-colored throw pillows (Wood), and have black accents throughout the bedroom (Water) in the form of picture frames, jewelry boxes, figurines, etc.

To elementally balance a small area such as a shelf: Place a plant in a light colored pot (Wood and Metal) and a square yellow candle (Fire and Earth) on a black mat (Water), and you have a balanced area. Add a few river stones (Earth) or a crystal (Water) to make it aesthetically pleasing to you.

When you combine all the elements in one place, the cycles, both creative and destructive, are working in harmony so that the area you are balancing is complete and whole.

Elemental Use: Method Number Two

Use one element to mitigate conflict

When two conflicting elements dominate an area or a room, use the supporting element to create harmony. A classic example is the kitchen, where there is an abundance of Fire (stove) and Water (sink). Since water puts out fire, add the Wood element to the kitchen in the form of plants, green towels, or a green rug to balance the Fire/Water conflict.

Another example is a living room that contains predominantly Earth and Wood elements. Let's say it has a wood floor that is brown (Earth and Wood), a tan sofa set (Earth), square wooden coffee and end tables (Wood and Earth), pecan-tinted walls (Earth) and lots of plants (Wood). What can you do to create balance? All you need are some Fire elements. Add some red or burgundy throw pillows, lampshades in fire colors, a bowl of red apples, a vase of red flowers, or some red candles.

This mitigates the Earth/Wood conflict, as the Wood can now feed the Fire and the Fire will support the Earth in the constructive cycle.

Elemental Use: Method Number Three

Use one element to strengthen

You can use a specific element in order to add more of that energy to your life. Let's say you are beginning a new job or embarking on a new project. You want this to move forward in the best possible way with the least number of obstacles. Purchase a brand-new plant (silk is fine, as long as it looks real) to strengthen the Wood element and remind you of the qualities of wood: growth, strength, vitality, flexibility, and creativity.

If you want to leave your current job but just can't seem to find the courage to do it, use the element of Fire. Purchase or group together the Fire elements you have around the home to harness the energy of boldness, expansion, inspiration, and authenticity.

If your children seem to be easily distracted and not able to focus, add more Earth energy to ground them. Place Earth items in plain sight to represent stability, balance, grounding, and nurturing.

Elemental Use: Method Number Four

Use one element to enhance certain areas of your life

In the next chapter, you will learn about the bagua, which is an energetic map of your home that depicts various areas of your life. Each area has an element associated with it. You can use the elemental representations that you learned about in this chapter to enhance specific areas of your life.

For example, you will learn that there is a specific area of your home that correlates to your knowledge and inner wisdom. If you have a big decision coming up and want to make sure that your intellect functions at its highest capacity, you can use the element of Earth (which you will learn is associated with that area) to enhance your decision-making energy.

If this area is your home office, you may decide to purchase an earth colored area rug to put in the middle of the room, or a big square yellow candle (Fire supports Earth) to put on your filing cabinet.

Molly had heard of the elements before, but she had never quite understood how they related to anything. She was finding this chapter very informative and useful. She decided that she liked the idea of having all the elements around to form the creative cycle and bring balance.

As she looked around, she saw that her home seemed to have a little of all the elements — except fire. She had no fire colors, no pointy items, and no candles. Some of her lamps even had burned-out bulbs! She knew she would need fire to get herself going and complete the cycle, and also to create flowing energy for the business she wanted to begin: Molly's Matchmaking Magic!

She got out her notebook and made a few notes:

Purchase red candles, red throw pillows for the sofa, and light bulbs for the lamps.

LIFEWORK

The qualities and traits of the five elements not only exist around us in nature, they also exist within us. Due to the innate expression of your personality, your past and present circumstances, and your complex life experiences, however, you will tend to identify with certain elemental qualities more than others.

Look back on your life and you may notice that you expressed one element more than another at different phases of your life. When you were in your twenties, you may have been bolder and more daring (Fire), yet once you had children, you may have transitioned into the nurturer and taken on the role of stable parent (Earth). Now that the kids have left home, you may find that what interests you is time alone, deep conversations, and quiet spaces (Water).

Each of us has all the elemental qualities and traits within. When we recognize this, we become most whole within ourselves. Answer the questions below to see what predominant energy elements you currently express most strongly.

The idea to create a series of questions about each element was inspired by feng shui consultant Mark Johnson in his article, "The Five Phases of Energy."

Action

Answer in terms of where you are now in your life, not how you think you should be, or how you used to be in the past. Use the following scale of 1-5 when you answer the questions:

      5 Yes! Exactly like me
      4 Yes. Quite like me
      3 On the fence/not sure
      2 No. Not really like me
      1 No! Definitely nothing like me

Don't peek to see what element you are relating to until the end!

MYSTERY ELEMENT 1

_____ Are you achievement-oriented?
_____ Do you like environments that are active?
_____ Do the hobbies you pursue tend to be competitive?
_____ Do you initiate things naturally?
_____ Do you have trouble with authority figures?
_____ Do you get irritated when others are slow?
_____ Do you like being first and best?
_____ Do you work well under pressure?
_____ Do you dislike constraint?
_____ Are you inspired by everything you do?
_____ Do you like to be the boss?
_____ Do you dislike compromise?

Yin-Yang and the Five Elements

_____ Are you always doing something?
_____ Do you like to pioneer new ways to do things?
_____ Is personal freedom important to you?
_____ TOTAL FOR ELEMENT 1

MYSTERY ELEMENT 2

_____ Do you think of yourself as a deep thinker?
_____ Do you enjoy things that are offbeat and unique?
_____ Do you tend to go with the flow when plans change?
_____ Do others think of you as quiet?
_____ Do you dislike people or conversations that are superficial?
_____ Are you creative and imaginative?
_____ Do you prefer to stay out of the spotlight and work behind the scenes?
_____ Do you find large social circumstances intimidating?
_____ Do you keep distance from others because you fear losing yourself in them?
_____ Are you predominantly frugal and conserve more than the average?
_____ Is the truth a primary driving force in your life?
_____ Do you have an interest in religion or spirituality?
_____ Would some of your friends label you as "eccentric"?
_____ Do you have strong concentration powers?
_____ TOTAL FOR ELEMENT 2

MYSTERY ELEMENT 3

_____ Do you like things to be precise?
_____ Are you always on time for appointments?
_____ Do you choose quality over quantity?
_____ Do you enjoy upscale and refined places, things, events, or homes?
_____ Do you have a cultivated taste for classical music, fine art, or upscale food?
_____ Do you worry about things not going perfectly?
_____ Are you someone who hates chaos and loves things to be organized?
_____ Do have very high standards for yourself and others?
_____ Do people who don't know you see you as cool and distant?
_____ Are you picky about things when you travel or eat out?
_____ Does your need to be in control drive your friends and family crazy?
_____ Are you a perfectionist in areas in which you are really capable?

_____ Do you have trouble when schedules and plans change at the last minute?
_____ Do you tend to own, purchase, or wear clothing that is light colored?
_____ Do you have a lot of clothing that needs to be dry cleaned and pressed?
_____ TOTAL FOR ELEMENT 3

MYSTERY ELEMENT 4

_____ Do you consider yourself pleasure-oriented?
_____ Are you a trendsetter amongst your friends?
_____ Are you just plain fun to be around?
_____ Do you love to entertain others or be entertained?
_____ Do others see your life as exciting?
_____ Are you popular and invited to many events, gatherings, and parties?
_____ Do you love attention and have no problem being in the spotlight?
_____ Can you get up and speak in front of people quite easily?
_____ Are you impulsive and spontaneous?
_____ Do you get bored when things are dull and routine?
_____ Are you extravagant in some ways and in some areas of your life?
_____ Do people see you as optimistic and enthusiastic about life?
_____ Do you have a strong aversion to pain?
_____ Do you love to socialize and get together with large groups of people?
_____ Are you always inviting your friends out to do something "fun"?
_____ TOTAL FOR ELEMENT 4

MYSTERY ELEMENT 5

_____ Do you love helping others out when they need a hand?
_____ Are you considered a nurturer and a caregiver?
_____ Are you a "hugger"?
_____ Do you consider yourself someone who is always there for your friends?
_____ Do you like to be in charge but do it behind the scenes?
_____ Are others usually waiting for you to finish or begin?
_____ Are you the peacemaker of the family?
_____ Do you love to be needed by those around you?
_____ Are you frequently let down by others or are your expectations of others frequently unfulfilled?

_____ Do you see yourself as conservative in your thinking and conservative when it comes to risk-taking?
_____ Do you like to belong to groups or be a part of a social organization?
_____ Do you prefer to wear cozy comfortable clothing whenever you can?
_____ Do you tend to put others needs before your own?
_____ Do you feel like you waste a lot of time and are not always productive?
_____ Do you always know what is going on with everyone else?
_____ TOTAL FOR ELEMENT 5

MYSTERY ELEMENT KEY:

Mystery Element 1: Water
Mystery Element 2: Wood
Mystery Element 3: Metal
Mystery Element 4: Fire
Mystery Element 5: Earth

Your Score

There is a low of 15 and a high of 75 points possible for each element. Add up your scores and list the elements in order from your highest to your lowest score. The element with the highest score is the dominant elemental quality in your life right now. The element with the lowest score is the energy in your life that is least present. Make sure you write today's date for future reference.

Next, add the scores from all five elements together and divide by 5 to get your average score. Subtract your average score from each of the element totals. The new numbers will give you a clearer picture of the degree to which you are expressing or repressing each element in relation to the others.

Remember, there is no "good" or "bad" element, and having one elemental emphasis is no better than having another. I created these questions simply to give you an awareness of which element is most present in your life right now.

Strengthening an Element within You

If you desire to strengthen the element within you that received the lowest score, use more of that element in your environment as a reminder to balance and awaken your inactive traits.

Consciously embody a new trait

Another way is to consciously take action aligned with the traits of the elements in which you scored lowest. For example, let's say you scored high on Wood and extremely low on Earth. Read through the Earth questions and see how you can incorporate some Earth qualities into your life.

For example, you could begin offering to help others more, bring lunch for your friends unexpectedly, give out more hugs, take your time when you are doing something, join a social group, and inquire more often about what is going on in your friends' lives. In other words, show you care! This will not only strengthen and awaken the Earth element in your personality, it will diversify your life experiences as well as bring a new sense of wholeness into your being.

Molly took the test. She had to laugh. She scored highest in Earth and lowest in Fire. Not only was she going to put more Fire elements into her home, she was going to consciously embody some of the Fire elemental traits! She knew she had it in her, but her fire and passion had been dormant for so long. Molly wrote:

My One-Step Fire-Awakening Plan

Seek pleasure for myself, create a life that excites and inspires me, and be more spontaneous, optimistic, and enthusiastic in my day-to-day activities.

This went right along with her purpose, she noticed. Satisfied, and with a smile on her face, Molly turned the page.

Chapter Eight
The Feng Shui Bagua

Defining Nine Areas of Your Life

By applying my three Basic Rules to your environment and looking at the balance of yin and yang and the five elements, you move tremendous amounts of unseen energy and open up new energetic fields that can bring your life into a greater state of balance. To take you to the next level, there is another feng shui tool I want to introduce you to that will show you how to direct your intention and energy towards specific areas of your life that you are interested in empowering.

In feng shui, every area of life and everything that happens in life can be placed into nine categories that are spatially represented by areas in your home. These nine categories make up an energetic map of a space called the bagua (pronounced bah-gwah). By understanding how this map relates to your environment, you can use it to engage your home in creating further support for your life.

From what I have written in previous chapters, I hope you have gained a new perspective on how your environment affects you. Now, equipped with knowledge of the bagua, you will be able to go to the next level by pinpointing which area in your home affects which area of your life, and learn what you can do to enhance specific areas to your benefit.

The Bagua as a Feng Shui Tool

The bagua is derived from the book of the *I-Ching,* also known as *The Book of Changes,* a sacred text of wisdom used in ancient and modern China as a divinatory tool. It is one of the most fundamental tools of feng shui and a powerful way to apply the next level of feng shui to your environment.

The bagua "map of energy" can be superimposed onto a floor plan of your space and guide you towards making changes in the areas of your home that correspond to areas of your life where you wish to see change.

Individual areas have unique symbols, colors, numbers, and associated elements that you can use to make enhancements.

The Nine Areas of the Bagua

The nine areas of the bagua are: family; wealth and abundance; health; helpful people and travel; children and creativity; knowledge; reputation; career; and marriage and partnership. There will naturally be certain areas that you will feel more inclined to enhance, change, or adjust, depending on what is going on in your life.

If you are having more challenges in a certain area of your life, it would be advantageous to initially focus on that area of the home or part of the room that it represents. For example, if you are having struggles in your career, then you would focus on the career area. If family dynamics are out of balance, then you would direct your efforts to balancing the family area of your home. The bagua enables you to identify the areas you want to work on and then proceed with a plan of inspired awareness.

Where to Use the Bagua

The bagua can be applied to any space that has a determinable perimeter and a main front entrance. The bagua can be laid over the outline of a plot of land, the entire home or business place, and an individual room or office in order to find the various corresponding life areas.

Use the bagua diagram at the beginning of this chapter as your guide or go on-line to the feng shui page of my website at *www.astrology-fengshui.com* and print out the color version. This diagram is what you will use to find the associated life areas in your environment. You can work with a hand-drawn blueprint of the space or stand in the actual space at the entrance, facing inwards, to begin. If you live in a dorm room, rent a room in a house, or have your own office, use it on your own space even though others may share the overall space.

If are laying the bagua over your home, you can also apply the bagua to each room of the house for a more detailed focus on certain life areas of interest. For example, if you are looking to increase your wealth and abundance, you could focus on not only the wealth area of the entire home, but also on the wealth area in each of the rooms of the house.

Divide the space into nine areas

The intent is to divide your space into nine areas, just like the bagua. To orient it correctly, use the perspective of the front door, as if you were standing there, facing in. Align the bottom line (the knowledge, career, and helpful people edge) along the wall that includes the front door.

If the space is square, each life area will be the same size. If the space is elongated, then the sizes of each life area will stretch accordingly. I will address irregularly shaped spaces later in this chapter. For now, just get used to laying out the bagua out on a simple space, such as a room, so you can become familiar with locating the various areas.

When standing at the front door facing in, the nine life areas and their corresponding locations in the home or space will show up as follows:

Family: Center left
Wealth and Abundance: Back left
Health: Center
Helpful People and Travel: Right front
Children and Creativity: Center right
Knowledge: Left front
Reputation: Back center
Career: Center front
Marriage and Partnership: Back right

Remember, the bagua is always positioned in relationship to the front entrance. Even if you use the garage door or a side door more often, align the bagua with the architectural front door.

Finding the life areas

After you have determined the front wall of the house as associated with the bagua, you will find that you enter the space in either the knowledge, the career, or the helpful people and travel area. To clarify, if the door is on the left side, you enter into the knowledge area. If the door is in the center, you enter into the career area, and if it is on the right side of the structure, you enter into the helpful people and travel area.

In this system of feng shui, these are the only three areas that can contain the front door. This means that you can never step into the wealth area or the health area when you open the door. Now, from here, determine the rest of the life areas of your home or space. The wealth corner will always be to the far back left (meaning the back of the house from the perspective of looking in the front door) and the relationship corner to the far back right.

Don't be too concerned about strict borders between each life area or what falls in the area. It is natural to have walls that divide the life area between two rooms or a life area that is an unused room in the house, such as a storage room or a large closet. And, although you may not think of the garage as part of the home, if it is attached to the home, it is considered part of the layout and can fall into one of the life areas.

Irregular spaces

If the shape of the space is square or rectangular, it is very easy to define the location of the life areas. If the entrance is complicated or the shape of the space is irregular, it can be a bit tricky and is beyond what I will cover in this chapter. In this case, I suggest you use the bagua on one of the main rooms in your home, such as your living room or bedroom.

If you have an irregular space and are interested in pursuing this further, you may want to look into getting one of the recommended feng shui books in the Appendix, which will contain detailed information and numerous examples that will assist you in accurately laying the bagua.

"Bad" feng shui?

Don't worry if your home has a complex shape or your entrance is situated such that you can't figure out how to properly lay the bagua: this doesn't mean that you have "bad" feng shui. It just means that you will need to get more details on how to read the space. Another way is to trust your intuition and see what "feels" right to you, and proceed from there.

For the purposes of this book, I am more interested in bringing to your awareness that life areas exist in the energetic template of your home. Placing visual and energetic reminders in the life areas (which will be covered later) will help to keep your thoughts on your intention, which is another way to bring yourself into alignment with what you wish to create in your life.

Where to Start

Now that you know which physical areas in your space correspond to the life areas of the bagua, let's look at each of the areas to find out where you want to start. Ask yourself these questions, and you will be able to see where your priority action areas are.

Family

Are you happy with your relationship with your family? Are you thinking of starting a family? Do you find that you are often excluded and yearn to be treated like "one of the family?" Are there arguments and dissension between family members? Are you unhappy within your family? Are you doing too much for your family? Are family get-togethers something you look forward to or wish you could avoid? In your business, are the employees and the managers getting along?

"Yep, yep, definitely gotta work on this area," thought Molly.

Wealth and Abundance

Are you spending money faster than it is coming in? Do you find that there are things you desire yet not enough money to pay for them? Are you in uncomfortable debt? Are you living paycheck to paycheck? Are there unexpected expenses that always seem to come up? Is your business profitable?

Health

Do you or someone living in the house (including your pets) have any major health issues going on? Does it seem that someone in the household always seems to catch a cold when it is going around? Do you desire to eat healthier? Do you want to exercise more? Do you have any complaints about your life that don't seem to fit in any of the other categories?

Molly reflected that her own health was definitely an area she needed to work on. She felt fat and out-of-shape and she was not eating a healthy diet.

Helpful People and Travel

Do you have trouble finding people to help you? When you need a ride to the airport or a helping hand with home repairs or even someone to give you advice, are people elusive? Do you travel more or less than you would ideally like to? Do you feel you have more than average hassles when you are driving, in the form of time delays, rude drivers, or car breakdowns?

Children and Creativity

Do you want to have children or are you having trouble conceiving? Are you having challenges with your existing children? Do you want to have more creativity in your life? Are you feeling burnt out by what is going on or stuck in a rut that you would like to get out of? Do you desire movement in a new direction?

Knowledge

Do you feel that you make decisions and then later you wish you had decided otherwise? Is there something you want to learn that for whatever reason you have not been able to? Do you want to change what you do for a living but don't yet have the wisdom as how you will do this? Is school challenging? Are you making what you feel are bad decisions in business?

Reputation

Do you feel that people mistake you instead of seeing who you "really" are? Is anyone speaking poorly of you and causing you grief or hurt feelings? Do you need courage to begin a new project or take a direction in life? Would you like more word-of-mouth referrals for your business?

Career

Are you working at a job you love? Are there obstacles in the form of people or situations at work that you would like to dissolve? Are you between jobs? Do you want to change jobs? Do you desire a higher-paying job? Is your boss over-challenging you? Are you looking for a promotion? Do you want to get along better with co-workers? Do you want to start a new business?

Molly felt a big yes for enhancing this area, especially in light of her new business idea.

Marriage and Partnership

Are you fulfilled in your current relationship? Are you lacking a significant other and desire one? Do you feel as though your current relationship is draining you? Do you feel that your current relationship has lost the luster of its early years?

Molly felt another yes for enhancing this area. She knew she would love to create a better space that led to a stronger partnership between her and Mackie. She began to make some notes in her notebook so later she could find the areas of her home that these life areas corresponded to.

Did you see a few life areas that you would like to improve? Keep them in mind as you go through the next pages, in which you will find specific information and greater detail on how to bring some new energy to those areas of your home.

Adjusting the Areas of Your Home Using the Bagua

Each area of the bagua has various elements, colors, and symbols associated with it. You can choose to apply any of these options to the space that you want to enhance. Remember, everything is energetic, every area of the bagua is connected to every other area, and no one area is more important than another; it is the combination of all that contributes to the complete picture of your life. It is up to you to choose what areas you want to bring into a greater state of balance.

Keep in mind that some energetic overlap exists between the areas. For example, although you may think to just enhance the wealth area because it specifically relates to finances, don't forget to look at where your finances come from. If they come from your career, make sure you pay attention to that life area as well. If they come from a spouse who works to support the whole family, you may want to put some attention on the marriage area. If you receive passive income from a product line you have created, then you'll want to make sure your reputation area is in balance.

Remember the three Basic Rules

To fully reap the benefits of positive energetic flow, do your best to incorporate the three Basic Rules you learned about in Chapters Four through Six. To review:

- Minimize the clutter in that life area (to maximize the energy flow)
- Have only things you love around you (have reminders of your intention)
- Pay attention to the pictures on the wall (use images that portray your intention)

Color, element, and shape

Under each life area, you will see a few colors, an element, and a shape, all of which relate energetically to that life area, and you can use them in any way you like to enhance the area. You can use all shades of the color, so for red, you could use red-orange, coral, wine, brick, burgundy, and so forth. For purple, you can use lavender, mauve, violet, and other such shades. In this way, you can make adjustments that will match your décor and your sense of individuality.

Feng Shui Magic Square

4	9	2
3	5	7
8	1	6

The Associated Number

You will see an Associated Number listed for each area. The number comes from what is called the feng shui magic square, which the bagua was based on. You can use the numbers creatively in the various life areas to energetically and visually enhance your intention.

For example, in the wealth area, where the number is four, you could place four gold coins to align the energy to the magic square. Or you could put five sunflowers in the health area, where the associated number is five, to boost the energy of health. The concept behind using pairs in the relationship area (which you will read about in the life area information section that follows) comes from the magic square number two, which corresponds to that area.

The "Magic" of the Magic Square

The reason the magic square is considered "magic" is because the numbers one through nine are aligned so that the numbers add up to fifteen in any direction (by rows, by columns, or diagonally) and fifteen is the number of days in a lunar cycle.

A brief history of the magic square

Legend tells us that sometime between 2205 BC and 1766 BC, the Emperor Yu was meditating on the banks of the Yellow River in China when he saw a huge turtle emerge with a distinct pattern on its shell. Emperor Yu took the nine symbols in the pattern he saw on the tortoise shell and transposed them into numbers, and these made up what is now called the Lo Shu Magic Square.

Later, around 3000 BC, Chinese Emperor Fu Hsi was meditating on the banks of the river Ho when a giant tortoise appeared before him with patterns on its shell that inspired the current nine-square bagua layout. The markings he saw were the inspiration for the trigrams in the I *Ching* (*The Book of Changes*), a book that is said to contain profound answers to the questions of life.

The Lo Shu Magic Square and the bagua formed the foundation for Chinese numerology, astrology, and feng shui.

Enhancing with Intention

So, whether you use numbers, colors, shapes, or symbolism to enhance one of the life areas, keep your intention at the forefront of your mind until you have completed the enhancement. What is it you want to see manifest in that area of your life? What is your goal, dream, or vision for that life area? When you see that area every day, what do you want it to remind you of as you are living and interacting in your home?

Below, you will find information that will help you enhance the area that you choose. Be bold and creative and use the guidelines to inspire you to do something unique. Traditional feng shui items such as crystals, mirrors, flutes, and wind chimes have been used for centuries to activate the flow of energy in a space and also serve a purpose. However, it is also very effective to incorporate items that have true meaning for you.

Don't question whether what you are doing is "right" or "wrong." Assign the symbolism of an object by choosing it based on your intuition and feelings. Remember, if you love it and resonate with it, it is "good" feng shui and will serve a purpose for you.

Molly was excited. It was fantastic that there was such a thing as an energetic map of her home and that there were things she could do in her home to help her in her life. She immediately found four areas that she needed support in and that she wanted to pay attention to. She couldn't wait to work on her family, health, career, and marriage and partnership areas.

LIFE AREA INFORMATION AND GUIDELINES
Family
Roots, Connections, Elders, and Tradition

Location: Center left
Color: Green
Element: Wood
Shape: Columnar
Associated Number: 3
Represents in a home: Family (biological and otherwise), ancestors, parents, elders, and relatives
Represents in a business: Superiors, bosses, authority figures, managers, and employees

The Feng Shui Bagua

We all have our own personal experiences with family. The stories range from one polar extreme to another, depending on whom you talk to. Some say how much they love their families and how close they are, and others tell you that they can't stand their families and haven't been in touch for years.

This life area was considered of high importance in ancient society, because honoring those who came before was a tradition based on principle. Family was thought of as the source and the foundation. In feng shui, the family area is considered the base and a place of safety for those in the home.

By setting your intention and enhancing this area, you may see or experience:

- A feeling of increased security
- Improved family relationships with those relatives living outside your home
- Improved relationships among those living or working in the home
- Greater inclusion in family affairs that previously you were excluded from
- A deeper sense of being a "part of the family," even if you are not related by birth
- Growth of anything that you are nurturing in your life

Using green

This area can be enhanced using any shade of the color green. This can be added in the form of plants, tablecloths, frames, stones, paint, pillows, or photos. Anything that has green on it will serve to energetically enhance the family energy.

Using roots and wood

Strong roots are necessary to stabilize large trees. Therefore, roots are important in feng shui and are symbolized by wood. Trees add the energy of wood, so having a bit of wood or tree symbols and images helps to stabilize the family foundation.

Wooden frames are great for this area, as are items from nature, such as plants or bamboo. Items that are alive and growing are especially beneficial. Wooden products also work, so paper, wicker, and rattan are appropriate.

Using columnar shapes

Since the family area is associated with energy that moves upwards (think "tree trunk"), items that are trunk-like and columnar are especially beneficial, as this is the shape that represents wood in feng shui. Tall plants, sunrise energy, and any aspect of upward motion depicted in art or objects will fit perfectly here. Photos that are vertically framed are enhancing.

What to avoid

Certain elements and colors don't do well in the family area, so take care to see that you do not have too much white or too much metal. Metal chops wood (think of an axe chopping wood), and the color of metal is white. Do not worry if your walls are white or if you have a metal desk that you cannot move; just use some of the ideas above to balance the energy.

Other notable information

Water is beneficial in this area because, in the elemental cycle, water "feeds" wood: think how we water plants so they will grow. In the same way, photos of water (rivers, canals, ocean, lakes), fountains, aquariums, fish bowls, and anything depicting water is positive. Black is also the color of water, so in addition to green, use some black where you can.

If you are looking to start a family, this is an area that you will want to place your focus on in addition to enhancing the children and creativity area.

This is also a great place for family heirlooms, family photos, and anything to do with family. Make sure the photos of family that you display here were taken at a family gathering where you had a good time and have favorable memories of.

Important Note: If your family constantly asks you for more help, time, or energy than you are willing to give, do not display an excess of family photos. Photos are representations of the person's energy. If a person is crossing your personal boundaries, having "too much" of that person in your life can be draining, even though you love him or her.

Especially avoid putting too many photos of such family members on your refrigerator. Your refrigerator represents the female energy (nurturing) in the kitchen, while the stove is the male energy (manifesting). The refrigerator asks us to do nothing but "hug and hold" the food that nourishes us. When you use magnets (sucking energy) to hold the photos to the refrigerator, you "invite" the energy represented by the photos to partake of your energy.

I have seen this dozens of times in client homes: from grandmothers who love their grandchildren but don't have a life because the parents keep dropping them off without their "permission" to siblings or family members "over-asking" for help in their lives because they are in a tight position and feel that you have the energy available to support them.

Molly found this mind-boggling. Her refrigerator was completely covered with photos of her sisters and her mother – all the people who were so demanding on her time and energy! On top of that, according to the bagua, her kitchen was in her Family area.

Right away, Molly got up and removed all the photos of her mother and sisters from the refrigerator. She instantly felt better.

Wealth

Prosperity, Abundance, Blessings, Good Omens, and Finances

Location: Back left
Colors: Purple, red, green, and gold
Element: Wood
Shape: Columnar
Associated Number: 4
Represents in a home: Financial status, blessings, good omens, prosperity, savings, and expenditures
Represents in a business: Finances, profit and loss, and opportunities

Just as some people are born to "nice" families and others are not, so also do we see extremes when it comes to people's state of wealth. Some people have no trouble at all with their finances, and others never seem to have enough. Either way, finances are important to all of us, as this is our means of exchange for obtaining the things we need and desire.

Although most people associate this life area with wealth and finances, it also is related to the blessings we receive in our lives, even in the midst of challenges. This life area is not only about being on the receiving end of payments, but also about having the experience of "profit" in the form of health, good news, opportunities, or a positive turn of events. Gratitude for what already exists in your life is also connected to this life area.

By setting your intention and enhancing this area, you may see or experience:

- A raise or promotion at work
- An increase in the profitability of your business
- Unexpected money or new ways to save money
- More opportunities for which to be thankful
- Saving more money than ever before
- Fewer unexpected expenses

Using purple, red, green, or gold

Purple is a strong color to use in the wealth corner and is the color that is originally associated with wealth. Red and green can also be used, because these colors sit on either side of the wealth area and offer support. Gold represents actual gold, which is highly valued as a source of wealth.

Use an assortment of items, ranging from stones (purple amethyst, for example) to bedspreads, table runners, curtains, wall hangings, or anything at all with these colors to help you to put energy into wealth manifestation.

Using symbols of wealth

Place anything here that symbolically reminds you of wealth. Some examples are actual green currency or even imitation million dollar bills, a piggy bank, a change holder, a jewelry box, gold coins, (chocolate gold coins, for example). What symbolizes wealth to you? Exotic perfume or photos of luxury homes, exotic locations, or a dream car may give you wealthy thoughts.

Using water

This area resonates with water, so a fountain, photos of water, or even a fish bowl will symbolically place the energy of water here. Water is associated with flow and is a way to get things "flowing" in the area of abundance. Make sure the direction of water flow is pointed toward the center of the room.

What to avoid

Avoid dust, dirt, and grime here. It is important to keep this area clean, so do not let it get dirty or disorganized. Do not store your broken items here. (In fact, do not store them anywhere. Get them fixed or donate them to get things in your life working again. Keep trashcans out of this area, if possible, and if not, make sure they are emptied at the end of each day.

Avoid "lonely" wealth corners. If the wealth corner happens to be your kitchen area, make sure you have cupboards that are filled with some food. If you have plants that are dead or dying here, remove them.

If your bathroom is in the wealth corner

If your bathroom happens to be in the wealth corner, in addition to noting what was written above, make sure you keep the toilet seat cover closed when not in use. In addition, use items that are "uplifting" in the bathroom to counter the downward flow of energy that can easily escape through the drains and plumbing.

Such items can be in the form of pictures of upward growing trees or plants, birds flying upwards, or anything that moves your eye upwards. Hang the pictures above eye level so that people who walk in have to look up to see the images. This will help to direct the energy upwards.

Health

Balance, Centeredness, Unity, and Wellness

Location: Center
Colors: Yellow and earth tones

Element: Earth
Shape: Square
Associated Number: 5
Represents in a home: Physical health and well-being for all members of the household
Represents in a business: Health of the people in the business as well as the financial health of the business

The location of the health area of the bagua is in the center and touches every other one of the areas. As such, it affects all areas of your life at once. The health area is like the hub of a wheel where all the spokes pass through, connected not only to the center but also to each other. The center of your home is an especially important part of the bagua. The health area also includes any other part of your life that does not fit into one of the other eight life areas.

Your health is intimately woven throughout all areas of your life. Without good health, you are not able to fully enjoy your wealth, your family, your children, or travel. If your health were extremely poor, you would not even be able to work steadily at your career.

By setting your intention and enhancing this area, you may see or experience:

- Enhanced health
- The ability to make better choices to enhance your wellness
- A greater sense of balance in life
- A stronger feeling of connectivity to others and yourself
- A slowing down of the "hectic-ness" in your life
- A new sense of stability

Using yellow and earth tones

The colors that represent this life area are very appropriately the colors of the earth. These colors will give you a boost towards vigor and vitality and help you feel both grounded and connected. Yellow flowers always make a nice addition to this area and are a nice gift for someone who is feeling under the weather.

Using squares

The shape associated with earth energy is square, representing stability, balance, and grounding. Things that are square-shaped will enhance your health energy. Square tables, square books, photo albums on a table, or items that are box-shaped do well here.

Using symbols of health

Things made of earth, such as china, ceramics, clay tiles, and pots. Brick and stone work well, as do potted plants that are alive and vibrant. Fruit symbolizes health, as well, so a bowl in the center of a table is a good idea. Fire elements are supportive to earth, so a square yellow candle would be a perfect way to combine multiple elements of health into one item.

Using fire

Fire is a supportive element to earth, so using a bit of fire in this area can also be a bonus. A red candle, a bowl of red apples, or anything red will give the area warmth. The sun is also considered a fire element, so photographs of sunrises, sunsets, sunny days, or sunflowers would enhance the area.

What to avoid

Wood is considered a destructive force to earth because the roots of trees can dig up the earth and take nutrients away, so do your best to take away any large treelike items from this area, and avoid an excess of green. If you can't, one way to balance out the wood energy is to use its transformative element, which is the color white, or items that are metallic. Green leaves of small plants are nothing to worry about.

Molly looked up and saw that her dining table was pretty much the only object in her health area. She had covered it long ago with an elegant sage green brocade tablecloth and complementary olive-green place settings. However, she could hardly see the top of the table because there was so much junk piled up on it.

She couldn't remember the last time she and Mackie had sat down and had a meal there. Over the years, it had become the catchall for everything incomplete. This constant overwhelming reminder that there was so much to do was her excuse for not exercising or eating well. She felt tired all the time. As she continued to look at the table, she realized that she needed to clear it off.

She made a note of it in her notebook.

Helpful People and Travel

Friends, Heavenly Connections, Journeys, and Support

Location: Right front
Colors: Grey
Element: Metal
Shape: Round
Associated Number: 6
Represents in a home: Benefactors and people who help you as well as any travel that you do
Represents in a business: Networking and business associations, including vendors, customers, and clients

Where would you be if it weren't for the people who are there for you when you need them? I'm talking about everyone from your chiropractor, massage therapist, and the mail carrier to your assistants and the neighbor who waters your plants when you go on vacation. We all have people in our lives whom we appreciate and wonder what we would do if they weren't around. And don't forget the people who do the little things for you, like the guy who pulls out of his parking space at the store just when you are in the biggest hurry of your life.

Whether it's travel to and from work each day or travel to the other side of the world, this is the area that supports all movement outside of the home.

By setting your intention and enhancing this area, you may see or experience:

- Increased synchronicities bringing forth perfectly timed opportunities

- More help when you need it
- Minimized encounters with traffic jams or driving delays
- More productivity overall as help becomes available to you
- An increased ability to relax and accept help with a new attitude

Using silver, metal, and round objects

This area resonates with silver or metal, so anything with these elements in it would be considered an energy boost. Metal boxes, frames, furniture, figurines, shiny paperweights, silver audio equipment—you name it: anything silver or even grey can be placed here for increased harmony and balance of this area.

Using symbols of help and heavenly connections

Spiritual symbols do very well in this area. You can use pictures of deities that have special meaning to you, or statues of spiritual beings whose help you want to enlist. Create an altar in this area to honor the spiritual realm, and call upon your spiritual helpers to help you in your life and in your travels.

Earthly help is very welcome, as well, so this is the place to put the business cards of those you wish to call upon for help. Likewise, place the books of those who have given you guidance on your path. If you are in the midst of remodeling your home, doing something to honor the contractors and all who are helping with the project is suggested to achieve the smoothest outcome.

Displaying your travel dreams

Use this area to put posters or pictures of places you would like to travel to someday. If you are not sure how you will afford such a journey, be sure to enhance your creativity area so that you can come up with novel ways to finance your trip with minimum expenditure, or enhance the wealth corner with the intention of opening up the flow of abundance that you can save for travel.

If you are traveling too much or too little (for work, perhaps) and you want to stimulate movement in the opposite direction, use countering photos or symbols to create the balance. For example, if you are traveling too much, put up images of home and stability. If you would like to travel more, place images of the destination or modes by which you would like to travel.

Children and Creativity

Offspring, Evolution, Communication, and Expression

Location: Center right
Colors: White, metallic, pastels
Element: Metal
Shape: Round
Associated Number: 7
Represents in a home: Health, growth, well being of children, creativity, and clarity of communication
Represents in a business: Employees and all aspects of work creativity

"Children" and "creativity" may seem unrelated at first glance, yet they are paired because a child is the result of creation (creativity) between a man and woman. Creativity is born from a balance of male and female energies. Children represent freedom and creativity. Therefore, this area has everything to do with children and everything to do with your ability to be creative in every sense.

Children start out in life believing that anything is possible. Since creativity results from feeling free, if you are in need of a new way to approach life and need some good ideas to get you moving in a new direction, this is the area to work on.

By setting your intention and enhancing this area, you may see or experience:

- Getting pregnant more easily
- Having more creative ideas regarding obstacles in your life
- Flow in an area in which you are stuck
- Greater efficiency
- Enhanced communication with your children and others
- Improved relationships with your children

- A younger attitude about life and living
- An adoption process going more smoothly

Using white, metallic, and pastel colors

White and pastel colors represent the color of metal and can be used to activate your creative side or assist you in supporting existing children or in the creation of a new child. It is usually pretty easy to find light-colored items for this area.

Get creative

This is the area for creativity, so be creative about your enhancements. Art, music, DVDs, televisions, CDs, toys, games, hobbies, and crafts are right at home in this area. Since the shape for this area is round, you could hang round mirrors on the wall. This is the perfect spot for a unique approach and one-of-a-kind items and for whatever symbolizes that which you would like to create.

Want to start a family?

If you want to bring another child into your life, either through adoption or natural childbirth, place things in the area as you would if the baby or child was already here. Place things in the room that symbolize children. Use smooth, round items and avoid pointy, sharp ones.

What to avoid

Fire and the color red are not particularly welcome in this area. The element of fire, represented by the color red, is said to dominate metal (fire melts metal). The farther away you keep fire symbols from this area, the better. If you have a fireplace in this area, an immediate cure is to place a mirror above the fireplace to "cancel out" the effects of the fire dominance; or you could put a metal grate in front of the fireplace to add the metal energy to the area. This is an important aspect to consider if you are looking to start your family.

Reputation

Fame, Authenticity, and Others' Perceptions

Location: Back center
Colors: Red

Element: Fire
Shape: Triangular
Associated Number: 9
Represents in a home: Your reputation; how people see and perceive you and how they talk about you
Represents in a business: Marketing, public relations, word-of-mouth recommendations, and business reputation

Those who are unfamiliar with the core meaning of this area often say to me, "I don't want to be famous." The name of this area can mislead you into thinking that it is about being famous, when in fact it is simply about how you are known to others. What is your reputation in the community? In business? How are you known? Is it for your career? Is it for what you do for the community? Are you known as a good father and family man? What do you desire to be known for?

Your reputation is dependent upon other people and can help you or harm you, depending on your focus and what you want. If you are a business owner, having a reputation for good service is favorable. Think of this area as how others perceive you.

By setting your intention and enhancing this area, you may see or experience:

- Becoming more well-known for what you want to be known for
- Clearing of any past misunderstandings about who you are
- Increased courage to do something new
- A stronger focus on what you want in life
- More respect from others for you and what you do

Using fire, triangles, and the color red

Fire is the element exclusively associated with this area, so it will be advantageous to use anything that symbolizes fire, such as images of fire, candles, a fireplace, or even a bright light. Every element has a shape and a color associated with it, and fire is represented by the triangle and the color red. Using a red pyramid-shaped candle in this area would incorporate all the elements into one item. Choose things that feature the color red or another fire color to draw attention to this area.

A television is considered a fire item due to all the action and light on the screen, so if your television is in your reputation area, consider it an item of support.

Using items that symbolize fire or fame

Some things you may also use to represent the element of fire are a book of matches, images of the sun and stars, a picture of a campfire or volcano, or incense. Another idea is to place photos here of people whose reputations you admire. Place your trophies, certificates of achievement, or awards in this area to "get the energy" out of all that you are. These will help you build what you desire.

Using wood and green

Wood feeds fire in the elemental chart, so using wood elements or the color green will create an energetic shift. Plants, especially live ones, thrive in this area and offer a source of support for your reputational intent.

Using upward-moving items

To match the energy of fire, you may also use items that have an upward movement to them, such as images of mountain peaks, churches with tall steeples, and tall, strong looking trees. Consider using other likenesses of what you would find in nature, such as birds and plants.

What to avoid

Avoid water and black. Water is used to put out fire, so avoid placing water images or water features in this area. As well, do not overwhelm the area with black.

Knowledge

Skills, Self-Cultivation, Mental Empowerment, Inner Growth, and Wisdom

Location: Left front
Colors: Blue
Element: Earth
Shape: Square
Associated Number: 8
Represents in a home: Mental growth, problem-solving ability, and spiritual and inner growth

Represents in a business: Intelligent business decisions, decisiveness, data, and business history

This life area is more important than you may initially realize and is worth putting some energy into. It is possible to get overly focused on wanting a stronger financial picture, a better relationship, or a higher paying or more fulfilling job. You could spend a lot of time and energy on those life areas, yet underneath them all, clarity and wisdom are what guide us to make the right choices.

What if you attracted money but didn't know how to properly manage it? What if you attracted some possible Mr. or Ms. Rights but followed old patterns and chose one who didn't fulfill you in the way you desire?

When reflecting on a past decision, at one time or another we all have said to ourselves, "What was I thinking?" If you seem to make decisions that you later regret or you have trouble seeing the good that is right in front of you, then this is a perfect area to work on.

By setting your intention and enhancing this area, you may see or experience:

- The ability to make better life decisions
- Higher grades in school
- A greater sense of confidence
- An ability to absorb more life wisdom from daily experiences
- A greater capacity for seeing from a different perspective
- A deeper connection to your inner wisdom
- An increase of creative ideas for your business

Using the color blue

Since blue represents knowledge, using blue in some way is beneficial for enhancing this area that is related to wisdom. Use blue as a general color scheme or as accents.

Using things that remind you of wisdom

Books and bookshelves are excellent for this area. Images that symbolize wisdom to you, such as people you admire for their mental capacity or animals known for their large brain capacities, such as whales and dolphins, work well. Use figurines and display items that have deep meaning for you or are inspirational in some way.

Some people meditate to find their personal connection to their inner wisdom, so making this area a meditation area, or placing items that remind you of peace and depth, will boost the energy.

Are there things you would like to learn? Is there a skill you want to acquire or classes you want to take but haven't found time for? Place reminders of them here to enhance such expansion.

Using water

Due to the location of this area in the bagua, you can use water to invite wisdom to flow towards you. Black symbolizes the element of water, so if blue is not appropriate or if you have items that are black, assign them with the intention of wisdom flowing towards you.

Clearing clutter to gain clarity

When you need to make a big decision, it is important to be as clear as possible so that you can make a decision of the highest order. Clearing out clutter in the knowledge area will add positively to the process of choosing the best path.

Remove items from this area that symbolize cloudiness, such as alcohol, drugs, and cigarettes (smoke). Get rid of old newspapers because of the symbolism of the news they portray. News articles are usually about disasters, people who have done things they regret, and other not-so-positive topics.

Using mountains

This area is related to mountain energy. Photos, posters, artwork, and wall hangings that depict mountains represent knowledge energy. Mountains in this area remind me of wise old sages who meditated in the mountains to gain inner wisdom.

Career

Life Path, Vocation, Business, and Purpose

Location: Center front
Color: Black

Element: Water
Shape: Undulating
Associated Number: 1
Represents in a home: Your life path, career success and direction, how you make a living
Represents in a business: The business itself and the growth and expansion of the business

The career area is one of the more popular life areas that I am asked to work on, especially for those who are not yet retired. Anyone can benefit by opening up new possibilities and potentials, whether to enhance what is already going on in a career or to explore the possibilities of an expanded direction or a new career.

Are you at a point in your life where you want to change directions in your life path? Begin something new? Let go of what exists in your day-to-day work life? Go from working for someone to working for yourself? If so, this is the area to pay attention to.

By setting your intention and enhancing this area, you may see or experience:

- Opportunities for a new job
- New inspiration in your current work
- Higher profits in your business
- Opportunities to change the direction of your career path
- An unexpected or overdue promotion or raise

Using water to create flow

Fountains are used in feng shui because they include both the element of water and a movement that symbolizes a flow of abundance and ease in your career or life path. If you decide to use a fountain in your career area or anywhere in your home (just avoid the reputation and marriage and partnership areas), the most important thing to remember is to make sure it is in good working order. If the design of the fountain is such that there is a direction to the flow of water, position the fountain so that it flows in towards the room.

In addition to a fountain, other water elements you can use are an aquarium or fish bowl; or an image, photo, or poster of the ocean, a river, or a waterfall. If the entrance to your home is in the career area and it opens into a hallway where you want to hang an image, make sure that if the image has a "direction," it points toward the interior of the house. In other words, to assist in bringing in the energy, make sure that the dolphins are swimming into the home, the river is flowing into the home, or the wave is moving into the home.

Using undulating and wavy shapes

In addition to symbolic water items, use irregular or freeform shapes to represent water. Avoid too many square-shaped items here, since square represents the earth element, which stops the flow of water. That would work against the intention and energy of the career area.

Using mirrors and glass

Mirrors and glass represent the energy of water and can be used in the career area. They work by energetically reflecting photons, which create a movement of light and consequently brighten up the space. Glass items such as vases, bowls, crystal figurines, glass paperweights, or frames all match this area.

Note: When you hang your mirrors, make sure that everyone in the house can see themselves without seeing the image of their head getting cut off.

Career-activation ideas

Place objects here that represent your work contributions and accomplishments. Are you just "working" until the opportunity comes to change into a career that you really love? If so, place symbols of what you would like to be doing. Use wall hangings that represent to you a better job or business opportunity. This could simply be images of happy people, which remind you of being happy at work.

The career area was one Molly wanted to focus on. She had figured out that, according to the bagua, her home's career area was right at the entrance. She wrote in her notebook that she wanted to set up the fountain she got a few Christmases ago, retrieve from the garage the ocean art that she and Mackie had got on their honeymoon in Hawaii, and put out a new welcome mat.

She needed all the help she could get if she was going to move forward with her new business and be successful. She could hardly wait. There was so much to do, yet the funny thing was that she didn't feel overwhelmed. She felt inspired.

Marriage and Partnership

Marriage, Relationships, Partners, and Emotional Ties

Location: Back right
Colors: Pink
Element: Earth
Associated Number: 2
Shape: Square
Represents in a home: The status of your marriage or relationship with your significant other, or desire for a partner
Represents in a business: The primary business partnerships, both internal and external

We learn about ourselves through our interactions with others, whether those relationships are intimate, professional, or platonic. As well, we learn to give and receive through the many relationships in our lives. This is the area people focus on when they are looking for the right partner or when they want to improve existing relationships.

If you feel you are fine as you are and don't need a partner, just keep this area balanced and clear to hold the relationships you do have in a good space.

By setting your intention and enhancing this area, you may see or experience:

- An enhanced primary relationship
- A better understanding with everyone you have a relationship with
- A business partner you have been searching for

- Finding Mr. or Ms. Right
- A new level of commitment in your existing relationship

Using the color and feel of love

The colors of the relationship area are "romantic" colors, such as pink, red, mauve, coral, etc., and the feel you want to go for is soft, sensual, smooth, satiny, and fresh. Anything that reminds you of romance and love is ideal. If these colors are not your style, use an accent piece or place one thing in this area that links you to what you want to manifest in a relationship.

The bedroom

Apply the information here in the bedroom, too, regardless of where it is in the bagua. Avoid fountains in the marriage area or the bedroom, because they tend to move emotions excessively. If you really must have one here, make sure to place ample plants around it so that the water energetically "feeds" the plants to create stability.

Using symbols of romance and pairs of items

Use mirrors, figurines, candles, fresh flowers, and anything that reminds you of love to boost the energy of this area. Put a lot of focus on pairs, and remove anything that looks lonely. Pairs can come in the form of sculptures, paintings, and other images, matching nightstands, two candles, two lamps, matching pillows, salt-and-pepper shakers, and so forth.

Including a focus on your relationship with yourself

When you are looking for a relationship, it is also important to focus on the area directly opposite the relationship corner—the knowledge area. A good relationship with yourself brings forth your inner wisdom and can serve to enhance the focus of your intention for the relationship area.

What to avoid

Keep photos of in-laws and children and anyone not related to the primary relationship out of this area and keep the focus on the primary relationship. (If you are not looking for a partner, however, then it is all right to keep photos of you and your friends here to strengthen existing relationships.)

Avoid anything that is strongly related to past relationships so that you can "let go of the old and bring in the new." While it is not always feasible to get rid of your bed when a relationship ends, do what you can to make it look fresh and new. Purchase new sheets and pillows, use new accent pieces, and so on.

Do not store anything under the bed that holds energy of the past, such as photos or mementos or clothes from past relationships. These are best moved out of your home. If you must keep some things under the bed, place neutral items there, such as extra bedding and pillows—things that are geared towards rest.

Molly took her notebook into their bedroom. She felt fortunate that their bedroom was in the relationship corner. She looked around objectively with her new "feng shui" eyes and saw their faded blue bedspread from long ago, no matching pillow cases, no pictures of the two of them, lots of dusty pictures of her sisters and mother. There were no pairs, and the dresser was stacked with a bunch of junk. The room seemed kind of dead, not unlike her and Mackie's relationship.

She also remembered that she had stored all her father's clothes under their bed after he passed. Her mother couldn't bear the thought of getting rid of them and asked Molly to keep his things at her house. She had not been able to say no, and because the space under the bed was all she had at the time, she put everything there to keep it out of sight.

She now realized that this was not a good idea; the energy of her father was still present. She remembered the promise she had made to her father on his deathbed and knew that she needed to get rid of his clothes so that she could make her own decisions about what was right for her. It was time for her to take back her life.

She made some notes...

> *Buy new bedspread and sheets.*
> *Bring wedding photos and honeymoon photos into the bedroom.*
> *Donate Dad's clothes if Mom doesn't want them back.*
> *Bring the pair of doves from the living room into the bedroom.*
> *Put some plants in the room.*

*Clear out the junk on the dresser.
Dust and vacuum.*

Whew! Molly knew she had a lot to do, but interestingly, she had never felt better. She felt empowered in so many ways. Julie's suggestion to focus on feng shui was exactly what she needed. The weekend was almost over, but she decided to schedule time each weekend just to work on her inner and outer feng shui.

LIFEWORK

To get even clearer on your intentions for each area of your life, take some time to write out your visions and answer some questions that will direct you to specifically define what you want to create. Use your written vision to set your intention when you work on the corresponding life area. The life areas that you enhance will then serve as daily, tangible reminders of your vision.

Family

Your Family Vision: Write the vision you have for your family. What does an ideal family life look like to you? What would it feel like to have a family life like this? How would your interactions be? What type of communication would be ideal? How much time would you spend together?

Action: Knowing that you can't control the actions and thoughts of other family members, what steps can you take towards making this family vision a reality?

Wealth and Abundance

Your Wealth and Abundance Vision: Write the vision you have for your financial picture. What does your ideal financial picture look like? What would it feel like to have this type of wealth? How would you live?

Action: What would it take for you to feel financially secure? What types of assets would you have? Where would you live? How would you dress if you had the finances that you envision? What are you going to do to take one step towards creating a more aligned financial picture?

Health

Your Health Vision: Write the vision you have for the health and wellness you desire to experience. What does ideal look like to you? What would it feel like to have this type of health, wellness, and lifestyle? How would you eat? How much would you exercise? How often? Where? When?

Action: What specific things would you like to do in your life that will keep your body well so that you fully enjoy your body as you grow older? How much would you like to sleep? When and how will you begin to implement actions that support your wellness?

Helpful People and Travel

Your Helpful People Vision: Write the vision you have in regards to the way in which you see helpful people coming into your life. What does it look like to you? How would you feel if you had this kind of support from friends and people you know?

Action: The number of people you know is influenced by your social life. If you could have the most fulfilling social contacts in addition to your friends, what would they be like? What would a balanced social life look like to you? How could you create a broader network base of people?

Your Travel Vision: Write the vision that you have in regards to travel. What cultures and places would you love to visit? If you could go anywhere in the world, where would that be? What experiences do you envision? Would you travel in luxury? Would you have a plan or go with the flow? Would you like to travel with your family or friends, or do you envision traveling alone?

Action: What can you do to begin to make these trips possible?

Children and Creativity

Your Children Vision: Write the vision you have for your children. How does it feel to see them living this vision? What is the role you play in this vision?

Action: Knowing that you can't control the actions and thoughts of your children, what can you do to support them? What actions do you need to take now to be a better parent?

Your Creativity Vision: Write the vision you have for your creativity and your ability to think flexibly and outside the box. How does it feel to go with the flow? How does it feel to have new answers to the same problems? How does it feel to be able to see challenging situations from a different perspective?

Action: What can you do to start working towards being more adaptable to what life brings? How can you reduce the stress in your life? Who will you see to gain a new perspective? When will you do this?

Knowledge

Your Knowledge Vision: Write the vision you have for your wisdom and knowledge. How do you see yourself? What does having wisdom mean to you? If there is new wisdom that you would like to obtain, what is it and what would you like to do with this wisdom?

Action: Do you need more private time for increased reflection, contemplation, or meditation? What can you do to increase your wisdom so that you can connect to your inner wisdom for life guidance? What distractions do you need to eliminate? How will you do this?

Reputation

Your Reputation Vision: Write the vision of the reputation you desire to have in your community and in society. How would you like others to see you? What does it feel like to have this reputation and live it each day? How does it positively impact the other areas of your life?

Action: How would your best friend describe you to someone who didn't know you? Is it congruent with the vision you have of yourself? Is how you dress, hold yourself, live your life, and act congruent with how you would like to be known? If not, what are the specifics of what you will do to be authentic to the reputation you wish to hold?

Career

Your Career Vision: Write the vision you have for the career, life path, or vocation that you desire to experience. How do you see yourself in terms of your vocation? How does it feel to be working in a vocation or job that you love? What does it look like to you?

If you are working for someone else and are inspired by what you are doing, write the vision you see in regards to your current job. If you are uninspired and desire to have a different career or vocation that is more in line with your purpose, write about that. What can you do today to move towards this inspired vision of your vocation?

Action: What can you do today to start walking towards the vision you see for your career? Who will you talk to? What additional information do you need? How can you increase what you know in order to move forward? Write a 50 - 75 word mission statement that includes your purpose, your intention, and your vision.

Marriage and Partnership

Your Marriage and Partnership Vision: Write the vision you have for your primary relationship. If you could have the most fulfilling and loving relationship, what would it look like? How does it feel to have a relationship like this? What do you most expect out of this relationship?

Action: When is the last time you verbally or non-verbally, in words or in actions, communicated your love and appreciation for your partner? When do you plan to do so? What could you say or do today that would help your relationship move towards your vision? Remember, you can't force another to be or do something they are not, but you can take action towards creating a possibility for that vision.

Note: If you are single and are happy to remain that way, write your vision of your relationship with yourself. What actions can you take to make this vision a reality?

Chapter Nine
Feng Shui Hot Topics

Frequently Asked Questions

What are the rules when it comes to plants, mirrors, fountains, bed positioning, lighting, and color? Since there are multiple perspectives and many schools of thought on what is "right," these topics often generate controversy and confusion. Whenever I do a presentation, inevitably ninety percent of what the audience asks revolves around the following topics.

Now that you are familiar with some basics of feng shui, you may have some of the same questions that other feng shui enthusiasts have. Therefore, I compiled a list of nine of the most frequently asked questions I receive and answered them for you in this chapter.

#1 - How Do I Properly Use Mirrors?

Mirrors are a tricky thing in feng shui. Proper usage depends on each situation, which is unique; however, if you understand the function of a mirror, you can better understand its role in feng shui.

Mirrors can be used to:

- Expand an area to give it a more spacious feeling
- Energetically and visually "break" down wall blockages
- Bring the essence of nature into a space
- Add light
- Brighten up a room
- Energize an area by attracting new energy into it
- Redirect energy flow
- Strengthen an image

In feng shui, the intention you hold when placing a mirror is important. Be clear on what you are using the mirror for and why you are placing it in a particular location. Mentally "assigning" the mirror a role sets the intention and adds clarity to its function.

Entrance mirror confusion

Many have heard that putting a mirror at the entrance is good feng shui because it "brings in the good energy." Others have heard that a mirror at the entrance ricochets the good energy back out. So, which is correct?

I have a simple rule. If I look in the mirror and feel drawn into the room, then the energy is being drawn in, as well. If I look in the mirror and want to run out, then I know where the energy is going. Look at what the mirror is reflecting. Is it a pleasant image or an unpleasant image? That is the key.

"Blocked" entrances

If you have a blocked entrance, you could consider placing a mirror to "unblock" it. A blocked entrance is one that has a wall blocking your vision from seeing the full view of the room. It stops your movement and consequently the flow of energy. Putting a mirror on that wall can "open up" the space and the flow of energy.

If you are contemplating whether a mirror at the entrance is "right," ask yourself whether hanging the mirror there brings beauty into the space, or whether, for example, it reflects the detested messy neighbor's house from across the street. Your answer to this question will determine whether a mirror is right for that wall.

Using an image instead of a mirror

If the reflection is neutral or does not inspire you, do not put a mirror there just because you have heard it is "good" feng shui to have one. (I have met many people who have done this!) In this case, it would be much more beneficial to enhance the energy by placing a beautiful image in the space, one that has "perspective" to it.

An image with perspective and depth will energetically "break down" the wall blockage and allow your vision to flow into the image, thereby creating a greater feeling of openness. Images that depict scenery or a landscape have visual depth and are the best choice. You can take it one step further by selecting an image that has a "direction" to it. If the image guides your eyes into the room instead of back out the door, it is even more favorable.

Basic mirror rules

Use a high-quality mirror. A mirror that warps images (usually a low-quality mirror) sends warped energy into the environment. Avoid mirrors that have ripples, distortions, cracks, or flaws, as they can have unpleasant subconscious effects. Also, avoid using darkened, smoked, crackled, or tile mirrors, since they reflect images with those kinds of energy. Since mirrors symbolize clarity and self-image, be conscious of the mirror energy that you place around you.

- Do not break up the image of anyone living in the house. People who are tall enough to look into the mirror must be able to see their whole heads, not just half their heads.

- Use an appropriately sized mirror. The larger the mirror, the stronger the energy. Bigger is not always better when it comes to mirrors. Have you noticed that people who have lots of mirrors in their homes have a tendency to be egocentric? People with low self-esteem, on the other hand, tend to have almost no mirrors, except in the most basic areas.

Is it "bad" to have mirrors in a bedroom?

There is not a simple "yes" or "no" answer to this question. If a client asks me this, the first thing I ask is how they are sleeping. If they sleep fine and wake up feeling refreshed, then no matter how many mirrors they have or where they are placed, they are not being adversely affected by them, and there is no need to take the mirrors out.

If they report that they have trouble sleeping and I notice a lot of mirrors in the bedroom (often in the form of mirrored closets), I explain that mirrors naturally increase photon activity, which in turn increases the vibratory energy, brightness, and unseen movement in a room. Since rest and rejuvenation are the purpose of a bedroom, having too many mirrors creates too much "exciting" energy, and that is not conducive to rest and rejuvenation. People who are light sleepers are often sensitive to heavy mirror energy.

A good solution for curing this without having to remove the mirrors is to install a simple curtain rod over the mirrors and hang sheer curtains that, when closed, will "quiet down" the mirror energy. During the day, the curtains can be pushed open to conveniently reveal the mirrors for use.

What if I can see myself when lying in bed?

The reason it is not considered favorable to see yourself while you are lying in bed is because, when you are sleeping, there is still a part of you that is aware of and "sensing" your environment. In the same way that light sleepers will wake up when they hear unusual sounds at night that others may not notice, sensitive sleepers will detect movement. Since we naturally move around in our sleep, this sometimes keeps the sleeper in a lighter phase of slumber because he or she does not realize that the movement being detected is self-generated.

An easy cure is to hang fabric over the mirror at night, or to angle the mirror (if it is a stand-alone), so that you cannot see your own reflection while lying in bed.

Mirrors and children's rooms

Children naturally have a high level of energy and are easily excited. My recommendation is to have no mirrors or only one in a child's room, as it is hard enough to get them to calm down each night as it is.

I once consulted with a woman who had decorated her son's room with mirror tile on the ceiling and mirror designs along one wall. It was done with an artistic and creative intent and her five-year-old son enjoyed playing with his reflection in the mirror during the day, however her main complaint was that it was difficult to get him to calm down at night. Once I explained the energy of the mirrors, she decided to redecorate the room with a new theme and took out the mirrors. She emailed later to say that it made a big difference. Her son calmed down at night, although it took a little while to take effect.

When removing mirror energy, give it some time to take effect

When you remove mirror energy from your bedroom because you suspect that mirrors are the reason that your sleep has been disturbed, do not expect immediate results. Your body is accustomed to "managing" the energy at night and will continue to do so for a while. It will take some time for your body to readapt to the new "quieter" environment and be able to relax more deeply. Give your body about twenty-one days to adapt.

#2 - Do I Have to Use Live Plants?

Grandmaster Lin Yun, the founder of the Black Sect school of feng shui, said, "If you have to touch a plant to determine whether it is real or not, it holds even more power than a live plant." He means that as long as an artificial plant looks real, it is doing its job. Your subconscious will see a silk plant as symbolic of a real plant, and it will have the same effect. Of course, live plant energy is favorable; however, it is much better to have an artificial plant that looks alive and real than to have a real plant that is sickly or dead.

Plant energy (real or silk) adds vibrancy and life force to an environment and symbolizes new life and growth. The best plants are full, lush, and vibrant. When choosing plants, select those with rounded leaves over those with spiky, thorny, or pointy leaves. Having too many pointy-leaved plants sends out a prickly energy, which your subconscious reads as "stay away." It is not a particularly inviting energy to have around.

Dead and dried plants

Dead flowers, dead plants, and sick plants emit the same dead energy into the environment. Even dried flowers symbolize death to the subconscious mind and can have a subtle impact. Replace your dead or dying plants with live ones for an immediate boost that can be felt immediately.

I am often asked when is the best time to clear out plants that are beyond reviving, yet still have some life force left in them. Many people feel bad about throwing away a plant that still has a bit of life in it. My recommendation is this: if the plant is dead, then anytime is fine. The best time to "recycle" almost-dead and dying plants back into the universal flow is during the three days prior to a new moon. The new moon represents new beginnings, so the best time to dispose of them is just as the moon is about to conjunct the sun in its waning cycle. This timing energetically gives the plants an opportunity to "begin anew," and we somehow feel better when we know we are getting rid of plants at an optimal time.

Dried flower leis and plants with meaning

If you have dried flower leis (Hawaiian flower "necklaces") or other types of dried flowers in your home that hold significant meaning and a special memory, then you should apply my Basic Rule #2: "Have things you love around you." If it is something you love, not something "dead," it is fine to have it around you.

If, however, such an item has begun to disintegrate and you can't remember who gave it to you or why you kept it in the first place, it has lost its positive personal energy and it is time to get rid of it.

Potpourri is often brought up because it is commonly used in homes and some are curious about it from a feng shui perspective. Although potpourri is made of "dead" plant parts, it does have life in it in the form of its added fragrance. However, once the fragrance dissipates, the dust settles in, and the cobwebs start forming, it is time to discard it. Some of my clients love potpourri so much that they do not want to give it up—and they don't have to. As long as it is kept "fresh," it does not take away from the positive feng shui of their homes.

Useful plant tips

- Move existing plants around to change up the energy of the environment.
- Fill empty corners with plants to create curves, fullness, and balance in a room.
- Use plants at the entrance to "entrance" the energy.
- Buy a plant for yourself when you need a boost and desire support.

#3 - Why Is a Fountain Considered "Good" Feng Shui?

Fountains are desirable in feng shui because they bring water energy into the environment in a beautiful and elegant way. Water represents flow, cleansing, sustenance, wealth, and abundance. Water in the environment reminds us of these things and prompts us to participate further in creating them.

Water was important to farmers in ancient China because their rice crops depended on having abundant water. Plentiful water resulted in plentiful rice, so water became associated with wealth and sustenance.

The role of negative and positive ions

Have you ever noticed how good you feel after visiting places in nature, such as the beach, the mountains, the countryside, or waterfalls? That good feeling is due to negative ions that are naturally present in the outdoors. Remember how it feels after a thunderstorm? That "clean" feeling is actually the effect of the release of a lot of negative ions.

Positive ions have the opposite effect; they cause us to feel tired, lethargic, and fatigued. Positive ions are found on allergens such as pollen, mold spores, dust, and animal dander. Electronics such as computers and artificial lighting generate positive ions, as well. These positive ions are suspended in the air, and the more we breathe them in, the more they affect us.

Water and negative ions

When water splashes, it releases negative ions into the atmosphere, and these bond with any positive ions suspended there. The negative ions neutralize the heavy effect that the positive ions can have on our mood and feelings. You experience this when you take a shower: you feel perked up and rejuvenated afterwards. Your feeling of refreshment is a result of all the negative ions pairing up with the positive ions.

No desire for a fountain?

If the trickling sounds a fountain makes do not resonate with you or if you have no time to maintain one and keep it running, you can get the same effect with a lot less maintenance by using images of water. If you are going to have a fountain in your environment, you must make sure it is working. Otherwise, photographs of water will stimulate your brain and produce the same energy, just in a different form.

Pictures of lakes or still bodies of water represent the energy of clarity, and pictures of moving water such as waterfalls or the ocean bring the energy of flow and movement into the environment.

Bagua hot spots for water

The best placement for water is anywhere along the front wall or the left wall of your home, business, office, or room and specifically in the following life areas of the bagua:

- Helpful People and Travel
- Career
- Knowledge
- Family
- Wealth

#4 - How Do I Properly Position My Bed?

Bed positioning is important in feng shui. No matter what school of feng shui you follow, it is a foundational aspect of the philosophy. How you position yourself in your bedroom has a relationship to how you position yourself in life, which in turn has an effect on how empowered you are and, to a degree, on how successful you are.

Gangsters know positioning

The next time you watch a movie that shows a head mob guy sitting in a restaurant, notice that he is always sitting in what is known in feng shui as the "power position." He positions himself far from the door and usually in the far corner, facing the door, so that no one can surprise attack him from behind, and he can see anyone who comes in the door.

Animals know positioning

In the same way, animals know to position themselves to face the door so that all they need to do is open one eye to see who is approaching. You will never see an animal lying so that, when he opens his eyes, he is staring at the wall or the corner.

Empowered bed positioning

Feng shui uses the same concept in bed positioning. Here are the "power position" guidelines:

Be able to see the door from the bed.

This means that when you are lying in bed, you need only open your eyes to see the door; you don't have to turn your head or crane your neck. At our deepest level, we feel most secure in this position. During the caveman days, they faced the entrance to guard the cave, because that is where a predator would enter.

Think of how a business executive positions his desk in his own office. He sits behind his desk so that he can face you as you enter his office. He does not sit with his back to the door, looking out the window, even if he has a great view.

Be as far from the door as possible.

There is likely more than one place to put your bed, and if you have a choice and it is aesthetically pleasing to you, place your bed as far from the door as you can. The best position for your head is in the corner farthest from the door if the layout of your bedroom allows it.

The further from the door you are, the more empowered the position is. Think back to the gangster example. The head mob guy could sit at other tables that allow him to face the door, but the further away he is from the door, the safer he is. This is because he has more time to prepare himself to fight any "enemies" who might walk through that door. Distance gives him an advantage.

Avoid situating your bed in the direct path of the doorway.

Stand at the entrance of your bedroom and imagine a bright light the width of the door shining into the room. Anywhere the light hits is considered the "path of the doorway." This path is like a windy tunnel of unseen, fast-moving energy. When you sleep in the path of the doorway, you have to work a little harder to "fend off" this strong flow, thereby losing precious personal energy while you are sleeping. It is energetically calmer to sleep anywhere in the room other than in this pathway.

A common misconception is that sleeping with your feet pointing at the door is "bad." In reality, this is a problem only if your feet are pointing at the door while you are sleeping in line with the path of the door. This position is commonly referred to as the "coffin position" because it is how dead people are carried out of the room — feet first.

If you have no choice but to position yourself in the path of the door, with your feet pointing at the door, then place a small table in front of the foot of your bed with a plant or large crystal that will help to buffer some of the energy so you don't have to process it all.

Avoid having the wall to the bathroom behind your head.

The bathroom consists of many drains, so the energy of the bathroom is draining. If you have ever sat in a bathtub full of water and pulled the stopper while still in the tub, you know how strong the downward pull of energy is. When you sleep with your head against the wall of the bathroom, the drains "pull away" some of the energy from your body. The most energetically draining wall is the one with the toilet attached to it.

If you have no other choice but to keep your bed in this position, place a small mirror on the headboard in the approximate area where you lay your head, with the mirror side facing the bathroom. You can purchase a four- to six-inch-diameter mirror at a craft store and use double-stick mirror tape (sold at hardware stores) to attach it to the backside of the headboard.

If you don't have a headboard, attach the mirror to the wall just below the top of the mattress to offer some support. This will energetically serve to deflect the draining energy of the bathroom. Make sure that you hold this as your intention when you are installing the mirror.

Consider the bigger picture

Some people position their beds against a solid wall because they have read that it is "bad" feng shui to have your head under a window. Although having your head under a window (more vulnerable) is not as favorable as a solid wall (more protected), it is far better to sleep under a window than to sleep night after night in a position where you are not able to see the door. If you have a window above your head, make sure to close the curtains or shades at night to cover up the "hole" in the wall, and you will be energetically protected.

If your only choices are to either have your bed against the wall of the bathroom or have your bed in a disempowered position, personally, I would move my bed to the next best position away from the bathroom wall, and then use mirrors and other cures to empower the position. Use your intuition to feel what is right for you.

More bed positioning details

Each bedroom has its own unique structure, so if your bedroom doesn't allow you to position yourself in the most empowered way, do not fret! There are multiple cures that you can read about in more detail in many of the in-depth feng shui books listed in the Appendix. They will suggest ways to use mirrors, crystals, plants, and creative positioning to your advantage.

My main objective here is to give you an idea of what it means to be in the power position. You can also use these same concepts when situating your desk at work or in your home office.

#5 - What Color Should I Paint My Room?

Color can change the entire energy of an environment and is very important to consider when creating a space that feels good. Color can change a mood, activate your emotions, and affect your subconscious. The impact of color is greater than just what you see through your eyes; it also has a vibration that affects you both physiologically and psychologically.

In addition, your reaction to color is cultural and depends on your traditions and your beliefs. For example, in America, people wear white for weddings, whereas in China, people wear white for funerals, so you can see that, culturally speaking, white means something different to you depending on whether you are American or Chinese.

Color likes and dislikes can also be very personal, so I tend to stay away from using charts that list what colors are good for the various rooms in the home. I prefer to work with my clients according to what feels good to them. Although every color has an attribute and a meaning in feng shui, it doesn't make sense to me to suggest that someone paint a room blue just because it's a good feng shui color for that room if the person doesn't even like the color blue.

Feng shui color systems

There are multiple color systems used in feng shui: bagua, five elements, and rainbow spectrum, to name a few. For example, as you read in Chapter Eight, the bagua color system uses green to represent new life and growth (the Family area), purple to symbolize wealth and abundance (the Wealth area), and pink to represent love and marriage (the Marriage and Partnership area). You can use these meanings as your intention when you choose colors.

The five elements color system, which we covered in Chapter Seven, uses the colors green, red, yellow, white, and black and assigns meanings to each of these colors. You can choose to use these colors to represent the elemental qualities that you desire to enhance.

The rainbow spectrum color system is based on having all the colors of the rainbow in a space to create a positive feeling in a room or in a home.

Psychological color attributes

Interestingly, the discipline of psychology also has a color attribute chart that provides information on the subconscious impact that colors have on people. Some of this is very similar to the feng shui color attribute chart and is useful when you want to find colors that evoke certain emotions. For example, the chart I have says that yellow represents joy and happiness, grey pulls down energy, and red provides energy and stimulates the appetite.

Bring in the essence of nature

When it comes to color, if you are not a trained interior designer with experience in picking out colors, I feel that keeping it simple is safest. Color and color strips can be confusing if you are not an expert, but by following the guidance that nature has set forth for us, we can appear as though we are experts.

My advice is always...when in doubt, use colors you would find in visible nature. Look at your favorite landscape image or go to the park on a beautiful day. The colors you see in nature are the colors that you can bring into your home without making a mistake. We never tire of looking at nature, so by choosing shades of our favorite colors from nature, we can create an environment that is based on nature's perfection.

The best kitchen and dining area colors

When it comes to the best colors for the kitchen and dining areas, choose colors you would find in the produce section of the supermarket. In other words, choose colors in the shades of the foods you like to eat.

#6 - Why Are Bathrooms Considered "Bad" Feng Shui?

As I mentioned earlier, bathrooms are filled with drains and are thought of as "bad" because of the idea that water, which represents flow and abundance, gets flushed away or goes down the drain via the bathroom.

While it is true that bathrooms are energetically heavy and are places where energy can escape, we must have bathrooms in our homes. It would be worse feng shui and very inconvenient if we had no bathrooms in our houses! Bathrooms can be "cured" or fixed so that they lose a minimal amount of energy. Of the cures listed below, you can choose to do all or just a few. No matter how many or how few you do, you will be taking steps towards keeping the energy from flowing away.

Bathroom cures

- Keep the door shut whenever you can.
- Keep the toilet lid down and the drains closed when not in use.
- Attach a small round mirror (approximately three inches in diameter) directly above the toilet on the ceiling. The mirror energetically "holds" the energy above the toilet so that it doesn't get flushed away. (The mirrors sold at auto supply stores are perfect for this.)
- Add upward-growing, "strong-looking" plants instead of droopy and delicate plants to counter the downward force of the bathroom.
- Hang a full-length mirror outside the door to deflect the energy. If you can't hang a full-length mirror, hang one that is half-length, or at least one that you can see your head in.
- Create a "wow" bathroom with your décor. This will help to raise the energy. I have seen Victorian, Elvis, cat, dog, and pig themes in bathrooms, as well as bathrooms with "wild" themes. If guests use your bathroom and come out complimenting it, they have helped you to keep the energy high.

Sometimes people who have mapped out their homes according to the bagua see that their bathroom is in the wealth area and worry that it is in the worst possible place, especially if they are having financial woes. If this is your case, do not worry. Just do as many of the above cures as you can to keep the energy in your home.

What bathrooms represent

Bathrooms are intimate rooms of transition. We go from dirty to clean and from no make-up to being made up. It is a room in which we let go of the old and release our toxins, as well as our tears. The bathroom assists us in processing that which we no longer want to keep within us.

It is the most private room of the home, and in public, it is the only place where we can get privacy. As such, the bathroom is a very important place in which to create comfort and support, especially when you are transitioning in your life and going through changes. When you are feeling vulnerable, you want to make sure that your bathrooms are protected energetically.

Bathrooms and color

Most people will agree that being naked is a vulnerable state to be in. Imagine being naked in a sterile white bathroom. Does the thought make you feel uncomfortable? White bathrooms can feel institutional and offer minimal energetic security and comfort. Remember, the color white represents metal. Metal has the qualities of being cold, hard, and unyielding and can transfer to the "feel" of a bathroom.

If you want a bathroom that is energetically supportive, choose colors that are deep and saturated to create a surrounding that is rich and enveloping. Creating more of the "womb" energy allows users to feel protected and nurtured while there. Earth tones, jewel tones, and deeper color values are excellent for the bathroom.

That being said, due to personal taste, some prefer light-colored, airy bathrooms and feel claustrophobic in anything else. In this case, just use a few accent pieces (area rugs, towels, curtains, shower curtains) in complementary earth tones to offer a bit of stability and warmth. Add images of nature scenes to bring in some supportive energy.

#7 - Is It "Bad" to Have a Television in the Bedroom?

I see televisions in the bedrooms of about eighty percent of the homes I visit. As we walk into the bedroom, many of these clients sheepishly say, "I know that I am not supposed to have a television here, but we like to watch it before we go to sleep." Many couples have this habit and are afraid I will tell them to give it up or tell them it is "bad."

So why is it considered "bad" in feng shui if so many people love it? This "rule" that people have heard about is based on the theory of proper placement and proper usage. Feng shui addresses this when analyzing a space for harmony and balance. Just as in nature you would never see a large oak tree growing in the middle of a bamboo forest or find a peacock running with the zebras in Africa, you would never consider putting your dining table in the bathroom, or putting your bed in the kitchen.

In the same way, televisions in the bedroom are not considered a "match." In feng shui, the more you can place things in their "proper place" and use each room in the way it is intended, the more balanced and peaceful the energy can be.

The function of the bedroom

The primary function of a bedroom is rest, rejuvenation, and intimacy with yourself or with your partner. The television is conventionally thought to be contrary to these functions. So is having office or exercise equipment in your bedroom, as it puts conflicting functions (movement and rest) in the same room.

Although the television can be a good source of information and education, another feng shui premise in regards to the television is that people typically get "lost" in it, use it as a form of avoidance, or find themselves distracted by it. This is seen to be contrary to the primary function of the bedroom.

Other television-in-the-bedroom theories

Some schools of thought believe that if you have a television in the room you can be startled by your own reflection in the television screen in the middle of the night when you awaken. Others say that the signal that picks up the stations is still energetically active even if the television is off, which can disrupt sleep.

Even insomnia specialists, who do not consider feng shui advice, recommend taking the television out of the bedroom to indicate to the subconscious that the bedroom is a place for rest. There is value to all these theories, but in the end, you must decide what feels right for you.

While all these theories do have merit, I feel that asking a client to remove a television for feng shui purposes if they love it or asking them to cover it at night if they sleep fine, is impractical. As well, I don't believe that you have to sacrifice anything to appease the mandate of feng shui.

What do you enjoy?

In regard to having a television in the bedroom, the most important question you need to ask yourself is whether it is right for you. If you enjoy having a television in your bedroom and it helps you relax, then it serves you and fulfills your personal purposes. It is important to reframe things so that you can enjoy a luxury or a necessity without feeling guilty that it is not "proper" feng shui.

If you need an excuse

If, however, you are looking for a reason to remove the television from the bedroom and can see how it adversely affects you, then that is a good reason to move it to another room.

When you and your mate have differing opinions…

The big challenge comes when one bedroom occupant loves the television in the bedroom and the other one wants it removed. Sometimes I am put in the middle of disagreements and am expected to side with one or the other and to tell them what to do. In a few instances, one occupant has asked me privately to tell the other that it is bad and demand that it be removed in the name of feng shui!

How do I handle this? I always allow the couple to come to their own decision and navigate towards the compromise that works best. If the television is staying in the room no matter what, and it is an issue between the couple, here are the questions I ask them:

- Can you purchase a cabinet with closed doors to put the television in so that it is out of sight?
- Can you cover it with a cloth?
- Can you mutually agree upon an earlier time for turning the television off at night?
- If not, can the watcher agree to wear a headset so that the sound does not disturb the other?
- Can the sleeper agree to wear an eyeshade to block out the light activity that may prevent him or her from falling asleep sooner?

It is never easy when we are at odds with our partners, especially when we firmly believe our way is right. Sometimes the one who is bothered by the television will just "put up with it," which leads to a build-up of resentment over time.

It is important to realize that the feelings of both parties are valid when it comes to how they feel about the television. Neither one is right or wrong. Even though no one likes change, both people must make an effort to maintain balance in the relationship.

#8 - Is an Asian-themed Look Necessary for Good Feng Shui?

This is a question I get asked quite frequently because of the way the mainstream has marketed feng shui with images of Zen gardens, lotus flowers, shoji screens, and meditating Buddha figurines.

Because feng shui is thought to originate from Asia, Eastern themes can and do come into play; however, at its core, feng shui is a nature-based philosophy that is universal. As I shared in earlier chapters, feng shui is more about our feelings and our personal resonance with our environment than about any man-made rules.

If your religious or spiritual beliefs include Jesus, angels, or the Ascended Masters, then place those figurines around you. I have seen fountains made of bamboo that look very Asian, but also resin fountains with cherubs pouring the water forth from a jar, which would be considered very European yet have the same function. You can replace lotus flowers with roses, Jesus with Buddha, and scenes of a bamboo forest with scenes of a redwood forest and still have "good" feng shui.

The bottom line is that feng shui does not mean you must use Asian décor; it means that you must use what resonates with you.

#9 - Does Feng Shui Go Against My Religion?

Feng shui is not a religion, nor is it a superstition. It is not something that you "believe" in, the way you believe in Jesus or Buddha. Feng shui is an energetic state that exists whether or not you are aware that it is affecting you. When a space "feels good," it is in a state of high feng shui vibratory harmony—often referred to as "good" feng shui. When a space "feels bad," it is likely in a chaotic vibratory state that people may refer to as "bad" feng shui.

In addition to feng shui being a "state of existence," feng shui is also a body of wisdom that we can use to create an environment that is supportive for what we want to create in our lives. The actual practice of feng shui looks at location, topography, building shapes, lot shapes, blueprints, interior balance, furniture placement, entrance accessibility, predecessor energy (who occupied the space prior to you), colors, elemental balance, and energy flow. There is nothing in feng shui (that I know of) that goes against any religious belief.

What is the difference between feng shui and interior design

While both feng shui and interior design consider aesthetics, feng shui goes one step further to nurture the people in the space by utilizing nature-based principles and honoring the universal energetic component that links everything.

Feng shui is based on the concept that everything in this universe is connected by an unseen energy or force called *chi*, which animates all living things. This energy connects human beings to everything, from the tiniest of atoms to the largest of galaxies. With this understanding, feng shui recognizes that, when changes are made in the home, changes are seen outside the home and in the life of the individual living in the home. This intention and understanding permeates all aspects of feng shui and sets it apart from interior decorating in this one very important way.

Questions, Questions, and More Questions

These questions are just a sampling of the ones I get asked most often about the physical environment. I hope that you saw common logic in the answers and recognized that, at some level, the answers sounded "familiar," even though you didn't think you knew the answers when you read the questions.

If you decide to pursue outer feng shui further, more questions will arise, but I want to remind you that if you are not able to find a source that answers your exact question, you are your own best source. Sit quietly with yourself and ask yourself for the answer. It is always there; it's just that our brains get in the way sometimes!

Chapter Ten
Empower Yourself

The Journey of Your Life

Our lives are amazingly complex journeys that never stop unfolding, always with new twists and turns along the way. The treasure of the present moment is realizing that you have the power to direct your life towards a new destination if where you are is not to your liking. Your journey is your purpose, and the purpose of your life is ultimately about discovering yourself.

Take a good look at your life and be honest. Are you currently where you want to be in your life? If not, take a moment to tune into your heart and envision the desired life you have spent time defining throughout this book. Make the commitment to point yourself in that direction. Even the longest of journeys begins with a single step. What is the next step for you?

Is it to rearrange the physical energy of your environment in the form of outer feng shui? Is it to look inward to your heart and use your mind to create new strategies for your life? Is it to become in tune with your spirit and your authentic self? Whatever it is, one step and a commitment to yourself are all it takes to walk towards self-empowerment.

Your Current Reality

Along the way, remember that it is just as important to focus on what is *not* there as on what *is* there. Do not be so locked into seeing your life and your world as it is now that it prevents you from letting go of your current reality and opening up to the new life that is in your heart.

With each step you take on your path, new experiences unfold. Be open to the possibility that anything can happen.

The Story of Sammy

Once upon a time, there was a frog named Sammy who lived in a well behind a small house in the woods. Sammy often had recurring dreams of a vast body of water. He would see himself swimming in it. In his dreams, he didn't look the way he did now—in fact, he looked strange—but he always felt happy when he had this vision of himself. Life in the well was okay, but it was nothing like the way he felt when he saw himself in this vision.

One day when Sammy was hopping around his home, he bumped into another frog, whom he had never seen before.

"Hi, I'm Sammy. Who are you and where did you come from?" Sammy asked the frog.

"My name is Richie, and I am from the ocean," the new frog replied.

Sammy got a good feeling from this frog and liked him right away. "The ocean? What is that like?" asked Sammy.

"It's big," said Richie.

"Big! How big? Is it as big as half of my well?"

"It is," Richie responded and added, "It's bigger…"

"Well, is it close to the size of my well?" asked Sammy.

"Actually, Sammy, it is even bigger than your well—a lot bigger," Richie replied.

"Even bigger? That is incredible! Can you show me where you live in this ocean that you call home?"

"Of course," said Richie, "but you will have to leave the well and follow me."

When Richie was describing his home, Sammy got "goose bumps" and brief flashes of his recurring vision of swimming in the vast water. Intuitively, Sammy felt it was time to venture out of the well that he had lived in for his whole life. At first, he was scared and hesitated, but his heart spoke up and told him it was time, and off he hopped with Richie.

Sammy followed Richie very closely as he led the way to the very top of the well, jumped off the edge into the dirt, and headed off through the woods. At the edge of the woods they came to a clearing, and Richie, without skipping a beat, hopped through an open field, over another hill, and then another until finally he came to a sandy beach. There at the edge of the water, Richie turned around just as Sammy arrived, looking a bit bewildered. They sat and looked out over the ocean.

"See," said Richie. "This is the ocean where I live."

Sammy looked out into the vast expanse of ocean that lay in front of him and exploded into blissful particles of light.

Surprise ending

This is probably not the ending you expected. You may be thinking, "What is the point of this story? I don't get it. Poor Sammy! He should have stayed in the well."

The point is this: when you do choose to take that first step away from what you know (the well) and go beyond the limiting factors of your life (walls, borders, or self-limitations), anything can happen! When you follow your heart, it is always the correct path for you, just as it was for Sammy.

The story of Sammy continued…

The blissful particles of light regrouped in the ethers and came together to form a beautiful fish that dove headfirst into the ocean below and was warmly invited to join a school of fish that happened to be swimming by. Sammy looked around at his vast surroundings while swimming with his new and friendly fish friends, wiggled his new fish body, and realized that he was living the dream that he had dreamed as a frog.

Moral of the story: Always listen to the voice of your heart. Any outcome based on a heart-centered choice will always be exactly what you need to bring you to the next level.

The journey of life continues

In the bigger picture of Sammy's life, his existence as a fish was just another step on his journey of life, one that he experienced until it was time for him to move to another level of experience. Any change you choose to make in your life by doing the Lifework in this book or enhancing your environment through feng shui will open up a new path for your growth as a human being.

Put Yourself First

Who are you living your life for? Is there anyone more important than you? Buddha once said, "You can search throughout the entire universe for someone who is more deserving of your love and affection than you are, and that person is not to be found anywhere." Put yourself first and any excuses for why your life is not the way you want it to be will fall away. The Lifework will help you to really see the importance of who you are.

Follow Your Intuition

We have all experienced having a feeling about something that later happens. When it does, immediately we think or say, "I had a feeling that was going to happen." Although recognizing it in hindsight is a confirmation of our intuitive connection to the divine flow of life, the goal is to learn to follow our intuition as our source of inner wisdom in the present.

Honor your intuition. It is your internal compass and develops (just like your muscles) with repeated use. It is your intuition that gives you direction from a higher level of consciousness. The more you learn to trust it, the easier it is to make heart-fulfilling choices.

Working with your feng shui at all levels will give you increased access to this divine flow. There is nothing more powerful that you can do to transform your life than to listen to your intuition.

Growth Has No End

It is in our nature as human beings to grow and evolve. It is also in our nature to want to grow towards the light of our authentic selves, just as the plants and trees grow naturally towards the sun. No one wakes up in the morning and says, "I want to shrink." Feng shui offers us a tool that we can use internally and externally on all levels to direct our lives towards our innermost light.

Feng Shui As a Way of Life

It is wise to look at feng shui as a way of life instead of as a "project" or a one-time mission to be completed in a given amount of time, after which you are finished. Learn the principles, for they are universal. Feel them, embody them, and as they become more and more a part of you, you will innately make positive choices in your life.

Congratulations

Congratulations on making it through the last chapter! Your interest in this book is a huge testament to the interest you have in changing your life for the better and taking it to the next level. Whether you briefly skimmed through it, plan to use it as a reference for basic feng shui information in the future, or have made a commitment to move deeper into the realm of inner feng shui by doing all the Lifework, you have opened yourself up to a new starting point for your life.

My deepest wish for you is that reading this book has awakened something within you, and that you cannot wait to begin creating your life in the exact way that you envision it to be.

Molly sat back and realized that she was not the same person she was only forty-eight hours before. Her perspective on who she was and why she was here on earth had changed so dramatically that she hardly recognized her new attitude about her life. So much had been awakened within her. Was it just two nights ago that she had sat with Julie, cried about her life, and felt so helpless? She had made a 180-degree turn. The old "feel-free-to-walk-all-over-me" Molly was gone. She felt the beginnings of empowerment deep within her being.

She shed a few tears as she began to put her things away. Molly knew that there was no turning back for her and that the journey ahead would be difficult. She realized that some of the things she needed to do for herself would create conflict and possible rifts with her family. She was surprised to notice that she felt okay about this. She knew that it was time to take back her life and stand up for herself. She was ready.

She had a long road ahead of her, but she could hardly wait to take the first step.

Molly Today…

Molly hung up the phone. She was smiling. She had just received some incredibly good news. Elaina and Barry were engaged — they were her forty-second successful match since she opened the doors to Molly's Matchmaking Magic three years ago! She'd had a good feeling about the two of them and knew they would hit it off.

She sat back and reminisced about her life and all that had happened since that time four years ago when she had spent the whole weekend learning about feng shui. It had been such a dramatic awakening for her that she had been relentless in taking steps to get her life back. "Boy, am I glad I did," thought Molly.

She had never felt better about herself and her life than she did today.

The Lifework was really her "life saver." Over the years, Molly had continued to work on it regularly in order to stay connected to her heart. She vowed to never lose that connection again. Whenever she feels she is falling back into her old patterns of pleasing others — which is often — she does her Lifework.

Her relationships with her sisters remain strained to this day. They never forgave her for "ruining their lives" when she announced that they would all need to share the responsibility for their mom. Although they fought her, she stood her ground. They had taken advantage of her for far too long. It was difficult on many levels and took her a while to let go of the guilt, but she knows she did the right thing for herself.

The extra time she gained from letting this and other "obligations" go, she used to work on their home. Today, their home is a sanctuary, filled with things that she and Mackie love. She continues to be interested in feng shui and has taken courses and read dozens of books following the first one. Mackie loved what she did, and over the past few years, their relationship has taken on a new closeness.

Her health improved because, as she felt less stressed, she eventually stopped her emotional eating. She joined a dance class and engaged a personal trainer once a week. The trainer gave her the activity she needed, and over the course of the first two years, she lost over twenty pounds. Her figure was back to what it was when she and Mackie first got married, and maintaining her health has become natural for her. She loves feeling and looking great.

The most daring and risky move she made was to quit her job. That took some time to get comfortable with, even though she knew she had to do it at some point. She started working on her business plan in the evenings, and she launched it on the internet about six months later. She worked on it on the weekends and after work and had a lot of fun getting it going. It wasn't long before she knew this was what she wanted to do full time. There were many challenges along the way, but she kept moving forward, and now the business is more successful than ever.

She turned off her computer and locked up her office. Tonight, she and Mackie were celebrating their fifteenth anniversary.

Life was good.

APPENDIX

Recommended Books

Feng Shui for Dummies, by David Daniel Kennedy

Move Your Stuff, Change Your Life, by Karen Rauch Carter

Feng Shui: The Chinese Art of Placement, by Sarah Rossbach

Feng Shui and Health, by Nancy SantoPietro

Clear Your Clutter with Feng Shui, by Karen Kingston

Feng Shui: A Practical Guide for Architects and Designers, by Vincent Smith

Instructional DVDs

Feng Shui Demystified, by Alice Inoue

Feng Shui Illuminated: Hot Topics and Frequently Asked Questions, by Alice Inoue

Office Feng Shui, by Alice Inoue

Schools of Feng Shui

The Feng Shui Way www.astrology-fengshui.com (Click on "Educational Offerings")

Feng Shui Designs Learning Center www.fengshuidesigns.com

Western School of Feng Shui www.westernschooloffengshui.com

Websites

BTB Feng Shui founder Grandmaster Lin Yun: www.yunlintemple.org

Practitioners

Alice Inoue trained practitioners: www.astrology-fengshui.com (Click on Feng Shui)

Feng Shui Designs Certified Practitioners: www.fengshuidesigns.com/pract/practhm.htm

Mary Swick: www.thefengshuilady.com

Note: All books and DVDs, along with more information on each, can be found and purchased online at Amazon.com.

ABOUT THE AUTHOR

Alice Inoue is a Life Guide who uses the modalities of astrology, feng shui, and spirituality in her work.

Born in San Francisco and raised in Taiwan, Alice attended university in California, then spent four years in Japan before moving to Hawaii in 1989. She started out on a path in business, but in an unexpected shift, transitioned into the world of media, first as a live daily television show host, following which she spent many years as a bilingual news anchor, spokesperson, and host of her own weekly Japanese television show.

Inspired by inner guidance and an awakening interest in spirituality, Alice made a bold shift in her life path and became an ordained minister. Soon after, she began intensive training in feng shui and astrology and has since developed a deep understanding of life cycles and timing and environmental space dynamics, which she uses with her spiritual wisdom to help people fully understand their lives.

Alice makes frequent appearances on radio and television and has been prominently featured by all major publications in the state of Hawaii. Her first book, *A Loving Guide to These Shifting Times* was published in 2008. *Be Happy! It's Your Choice* followed in 2009. In addition, she has produced three instructional DVDs in partnership with Oceanic Time Warner Cable, which covers popular aspects of feng shui.

Her expertise in all that she does also enables her to share her wisdom through private sessions, workshops, and seminars. It inspires her to help others awaken to their divine potential.

For further information, please visit Alice's websites at:

www.astrology-fengshui.com
www.peleoflemuria.com

Made in the USA
Charleston, SC
30 January 2011